The Myth of UK Integration

This book dares to say what the Politically Correct Thought Police are determined you should not know.
Michael Cole

If we fail to learn how to live with one another... it is inevitable that divisions and hostility will occur.
From the Foreword by Lord Noon of
St John's Wood

We Don't Need You Any More
The Myth of UK Integration

Kailash Puri
with Bob Whittington

Whittles Publishing

Published by
Whittles Publishing Limited,
Dunbeath,
Caithness, KW6 6EG,
Scotland, UK
www.whittlespublishing.com

ISBN 978-184995-059-6

An environmentally friendly book printed and bound in England
by www.printondemand-worldwide.com

Mixed Sources
Product group from well-managed
forests, and other controlled sources
www.fsc.org Cert no. TT-COC-002641
© 1996 Forest Stewardship Council
FSC

PEFC Certified
This product is
from sustainably
managed forests
and controlled
sources
www.pefc.org
PEFC
PEFC/16-33-415

This book is made entirely of chain-of-custody materials

Contents

Foreword

Kailash Puri has spent her lifetime building bridges, restoring broken relationships, and her gentle but timely book continues this work in the same understated style.

Drawing on her personal experience of more than half a century of giving advice to successive generations as well as different nationalities in India, Africa, the USA and for most of her life in the UK, she calls our attention to sadly one of the most divisive features of British society – our unwillingness to appreciate the richness of our diversity and as a result our apparent refusal to mix.

The success of some so-called ethnic minorities has done nothing to improve relations; in fact it has tended to have the reverse effect with inevitable adverse consequences. Equally the failure of some communities has been used as false evidence that racism flourishes in the UK.

If we fail to learn how to live with one another, and that does not mean existing in parallel worlds or hiding away in what Kailash Puri calls mink-lined ghettoes, it is inevitable that divisions and hostility will occur.

This book looks at real life through the eyes of ordinary people who are finding it difficult to make sense of our increasingly antagonistic and multi-cultural society; often the fractures are within the same community as younger generations challenge old traditions.

This is where all government policies and initiatives come into play on the streets, in the schools and homes of our country. Kailash Puri has written many books in her native Punjabi but this is her first in English and she has used the occasion to warn us that we must try to understand our differences and then start talking to one another before it is too late.

Lord Noon of St John's Wood

Introduction

There was discrimination on the factory floor, on the buses and trains. It hurt deeply, but we tried to ignore it, thinking we won't be here too long, only a couple more years until we have enough capital to start our own business back home in India. It was sheer hard work – dark cold rooms, not even hot water. But now looking back after so many years, I think we did not have as many problems, pressures and worries then as we do today.

My agony aunt's postbag is not only about sexual problems, it is also about concerns such as these. It reflects the minutiae of daily lives, as far removed from the corridors of political power as it possible to get and yet it is the very stuff of life. If law makers want to know about integration, or the lack of it, this is where they should begin their study.

This book focuses on the Indian population who over the last half century have settled in Britain and who, in large part, have been successful in all walks of life. But for the Indians, one could just as easily read Pakistani, Chinese, Arab, Polish, Bulgarian, Turk, Kurd or indeed any one of the other ethnic groups who have come to the United Kingdom in search of a better life. In London alone more than 300 different languages are said to be spoken.

Let's look at some numbers. According to the Office for National Statistics (ONS) the UK population increased more between 2009–2010 than in any year for the previous half century rising some 470,000 to an estimated 62,262,000 people. Interestingly it is the natural change, the difference between births and deaths, which accounted for just over half the increase over-taking net migration as the key element in the population growth. The highest recorded figure for people arriving in the UK was 590,000 in 2006; although if one includes illegal immi-grants and those simply missed by the register all these figures could be much higher. The ONS points to the rising fertility of UK-born women and the rise in inward migration of women of child bearing age.

In 2009 the ONS projected that the population of the UK would increase by over 4 million to 65.6 million in 2018 and reach 71.6 million by 2033. More recently the House of Com-mons library estimated that we would push through the 70 mil-lion mark much earlier – by 2026.

Soon after coming to office in July 2010, Britain's new coali-tion Conservative/Liberal Democrat government was talking loudly of imposing a cap on non-European immigrants but there appeared to be signs of strain even within the cabinet about how strictly that would or could be enforced. It was suggested that the Conservative wing wanted to see an immigration fig-ure nearer 50,000.

Migration between countries has been part of the world's de-velopment for centuries and Britain is by no means the only place where people from other countries have settled. Equally the English, Irish, Scots and Welsh have travelled to other lands themselves in search of a new life – it is estimated that three million emigrated between 1853 and 1880 alone in a bid to es-cape the grinding poverty of the slums of Victorian England. A record high – 427,000 – left Britain in 2008, but of those 255,000 were non-British citizens. The British have settled in America, Canada, Australia and New Zealand, but also in India, Burma, Africa and other more 'foreign' destinations.

However the Anglo-Saxon settlers of old did not have racial problems in those countries as they were regarded as the rulers and commanded, in their view, racial superiority. Needless to say there was no question of their integrating. They did not have to learn the local language or change food habits or even wear the ethnic dress. Quite the reverse in fact, the locals were expected to learn the white rulers' ways. Characteristically perhaps they kept themselves to themselves unless of course it was meeting the Maharajahs, Nawabs, political leaders or the business community. The English writer, Somerset Maugham, tartly observed the racial attitude of the colonials in the Indian Raj: *Even the working class British women who are nowhere near the intelligence of Indian women kept them at arm's length.*

After World War II and the Independence and Partition of India in 1947, Indians and Pakistanis came to Britain where they were put to work in the factories and foundries. Life was hard. Overworked and alienated by the British, they were lonely and naturally wanted their families to join them. These first Asian arrivals, the factory fodder, were recruited by the retired British army soldiers who had served with the Indian army during World War II.

These early years were devoted to work – seven days a week – often with the husband and wife working different shifts. One who became a millionaire in later life recalls: *When my wife stepped out of the bus in the evening, I boarded it to go to the factory. We were seldom at home together.*

Then the worm turned and it was the Asian population who, through diligence and intelligence, became the new wealthy, but despite these riches there is a very noticeable chip on some shoulders. Beneath the surface of often great affluence or even just comfortable middle class living the tensions are high; there is cultural conflict, alienation and isolation. There is also confusion in their minds. They want to be accepted both for who and what they are and yet there is, certainly among some Indians, an almost overwhelming desire 'to be English.' Not all Asian groups have 'made it'; some most noticeably the Bangladeshis are struggling at the bottom of the economic pile with 65 per cent living in poverty according to official statistics.

Pious words from political and spiritual leaders about embracing a multi-cultural world of inter-faith and integration remain just that, wishful thinking and wonderful ideas. Ideas without people will always be just ideas. If by integration we mean a complete mixture of races, colours and creeds living together in one neighbourhood, conducting business together, socialising together and even inter-marrying, then sadly we are dreaming. Integration at best will be living parallel lives in adjoining neighbourhoods in relatively peaceful harmony. But even that is a dream which cannot become reality unless all peoples make the enormous leap of putting others first in their lives.

Isolation does not work. It does not work for nations and it does not work for people. Nevertheless that is what is happening in the UK today. Quite naturally the down-trodden immigrant worker seeks solace among his or her own kind; the rest of the family is often encouraged to travel here if for no other reason than to give moral support. All too soon whole neighbourhoods are transformed and take on a particular ethnic face; every shop is say Indian owned, so are the restaurants; the banks are run by ethnic people who are able to talk the same language. In time it can become a no-go area for white English – there is aggression in the air. No attempt is made to integrate with the host nation and its people, no effort is made to learn the local language and the isolation becomes more pronounced. Local authorities encourage this failure to integrate with signs in public places in a multitude of different languages or by providing interpreters in the courts and council offices for those who cannot be bothered to learn English. It is noticeable that in places like Dubai with a large Asian population signs are in Arabic and English only and the Asians all cope by learning one or the other language fluently.

Pity the individual who wants to adopt the English culture or at least meet a white 'Brit', his is an impossible task in some areas. We should spare a thought for him. On the one hand he is viewed with suspicion, on the other he is vilified for abandoning his own kind. When I came to Britain, long before most of the British cabinet were born, I experienced and witnessed ethnic minority life first hand. My job was, and still is, to help people overcome their personal problems and at the very heart of so many of those problems is race. It may come disguised as marital problems, teenage problems, religious problems, sexual problems but it is really all about people not liking others; this is intensified when dealing with 'foreigners'.

Britain has not moved on. On the 4th July Americans of all colours and creeds put their hand on their hearts and swear allegiance to the flag and their country as Americans. When my husband and I were established in the UK I was given £90,000 to set up a Punjabi centre to celebrate my own heritage; it served only to accentuate my difference and did nothing to cultivate my pride in being English, which I was not. I have lived here most of my life and love Great Britain, but I remain Indian.

We should not pretend that we are becoming more broadminded and open to other cultures. The world we are told has become smaller thanks to cheaper air travel and yet for all that travelling there seems to be little understanding between peoples. The charter flights deliver passengers to exotic destinations where they spend a fortnight with the same charter travellers and return home with a tan but no knowledge of the country they have visited. Of course there are exceptions, people with a real desire to learn and understand, people who want to reach out, but they are in the minority and their voice is often drowned out. It was noticeable that even the former Prime Minister, Tony Blair, had to wait until he was out of office before feeling free to say publicly on television that radical elements should be treated more firmly. Those who know him said he had been restrained from taking a tougher line while in Downing Street for fear of rocking the racial boat.

One might have expected that the wonders of satellite television, the internet and the instant information provided to our very mobile phones would have opened peoples' eyes to the world around them, but incredibly the reverse seems to be the case. Today we do not have to look up from out laptops or turn off our iPods as we move about – in short we do not need to, and even do not want to communicate with each other. It is said we spend seven hours a day watching electronic media – TV, computers and the like. When I first arrived in the UK over half a century ago people did talk to these 'strange looking Indians', but that was out of curiosity. Familiarity it seems really does breed contempt – and that works both ways.

Another reason for such insularity is the mistaken agenda of the politically correct world in which we live; an innocent smile can be interpreted as sexual harassment or worse still if directed towards a laughing child or gurgling baby in a passing pram. Better therefore to get on with your own life, try not to upset anyone until you are safely back at home watching TV, broadcast in your own native tongue, surrounded by people who 'understand' you.

So if we dare not talk or smile at one another even among our own race what hope is there for a newcomer to our shores? A postbag of letters over the past 50 years or more brings constant tales of misery, and it is a misery which is now compounded, not alleviated, by growing affluence. Worse, it is a clash of cultures which not only is divisive among different racial groups but also within the same group.

For sure these again are extreme examples, but for too long our vocabulary has been soft and non-combative – we have forgotten how to call a spade a spade. At my age, I have not got time to mince my words. When my phone rings or I open my letters, I have to give straightforward, clear, uncomplicated advice just like any aunt telling her errant young nephews and nieces some unpalatable truths. The unpalatable truth about life in Britain is that its citizens at best are not getting along and at worst are effectively at war. What else do you call attempted suicide bombing? Yes, they are the minority, but the rest of us are not 'rubbing along', we are doing worse than that, we are ignoring one another, pretending the others do not exist.

Third and fourth generation Asian Brits are torn between the old ways and the new freedoms on full and vulgar display around them. Such friction leads to animosity towards what is seen as a host nation without morals, standards and discipline and so the division becomes wider. If you don't like it go back to your own home, is the obvious retort, but of course this is home. It is too late to return to India which either cannot provide for them or where they have lost all family contact.

So what is the natural reaction? Hunker down as the Americans would say. Gather around yourself your own kind; forget the whites, after all you do not even need them any more. Indians have launched their own banks, run major restaurant chains and hotels, operate their own travel agencies and airlines and have their own newspapers and media outlets entirely devoid of any English input. The nation becomes polarised into different camps. This independence means that most now simply ignore completely the traditional ways and culture of Britain. In short they are entirely self-reliant and with that self-reliance a certain arrogance is developing. We don't need you anymore. Why bother integrating?

The answer to that question is surely that we cannot live in parallel communities. Jealousies and envies build up, it is human nature. Just read the letters in the post bag; either the small ethnic grouping grows too powerful and successful or it feels downtrodden and weak, but in either case the status quo can never remain without some clear, often violent, conclusion. It is no argument to say the English are too quiet by nature to riot. Surely the mayhem of August 2011 – looting, arson and even murder have once and for all sadly disproved that cosy notion. The mix of cultures includes people from countries where resorting to violence, knives and guns is second nature and, lest we forget, not so long ago in 2001 the riots in Oldham were blamed on the growth of 'racial ghettos'. It doesn't take very much to unleash pent up animosity, hatred and jealousies and any excuse will do to respond to a call to join in wanton thuggery, circulated like wildfire on the mobile phone networks.

There have been repeated political initiatives in recent times to stem the tide of immigration to the UK and only allow in qualified people, but even if the 'right types' are given entry permits where will they live? Inevitably they will gravitate to their ghettos or colonies, however comfortable they might be.

The waves of immigrants undoubtedly affect the balance of a community and that has to be addressed if the social cohesion, as it has been dubbed, is to be achieved. I remember a report back in June 2007 by the government's Commission on Integration and Cohesion which outlined further measures to improve community relations including 'cultural briefing packs' which could be supplied to immigrants, providing information on appropriate behaviour. It was also proposed that specialist integration teams should be set up to support areas experiencing strains between minority groups. The impact of immigration has to be faced and it requires genuine effort not only by the host nation, but perhaps more particularly by the new arrivals.

These few chapters examine the tensions of every day life in multi-cultural Britain at an intensely personal level, seeking to understand and clarify some of the conflicts and misunderstandings which exist between the white English and their new fellow citizens of Asian origin.

The advice I have given over the years is not as some disinterested academic studying an interesting question of sociology, but as someone who has experienced the nervousness and then joy of an early marriage, the feeling of homesickness, the coolness of a community and then the warmth of hospitality and friends. My parents chose my husband, who was already on his way to becoming a brilliant scientist, when I was only 15. I was lucky and my marriage worked and became the source of my learning. We were among the earliest Indian immigrants, travelled the world together, always returning to England. My education was in the real world where I learned about people first hand.

Only by trying to understand each other's culture and traditions can we dispel the mistrust which exists between these two communities but understand we must because it is from these apparently benign seeds of disquiet and anxiety that eventually anger and resentment grow. The terrible bombings of 7th July 2005 on the London buses and underground did not suddenly happen, their roots could be traced back to years of isolation, racism, segregation and smouldering animosity.

The Asians, who by nature are hospitable, believe it is lucky to invite guests to their homes. A house full of guests is considered blessed. The British have invited not just Indians but many other races to their shores, so if Britain is to enjoy good fortune everyone, host and guest alike, must begin by trying to comprehend the sometimes mysterious ways of our new neighbours.

If the UK needs all the thousands of immigrant workers who arrive every year then we must decide whether they will be treated and welcomed as full citizens or merely factory fodder like the lady who worked in the cold, dark rooms all those years ago, hoping for a better future. If it is factory fodder then this will not remain a United Kingdom, it will be a Tower of Babel with all its failings. We will continue to throw out free welfare like Christmas presents until there is no more to go round, the social barriers will become barricades, there will be more no-go areas for the 'whites' and then the legendary English reserve will finally snap. Someone will say enough is enough.

Chapter 1

A challenge to family and tradition

There is no going back, every year, every day, Britain is becoming a more multi-racial, multi-cultural society and every year, every day we seem to like and trust each other less.

A recent study in England and Wales showed that about 9% of the population is of ethnic minority background and roughly half of those are of Asian origin. These numbers are relatively modest. We are hardly being swamped by immigrants, but it is what those immigrants do, how they behave, what they believe and what their traditions are which have a direct bearing on life in Britain.

We have to consider the norms of behaviour in the countries they have left – they bring that baggage with them. Some immigrants have escaped the harsh poverty of their homeland where life in inner cities resembles the law of the jungle; arguments and disputes are settled violently without recourse to the courts or judicial system which are often regarded as just as corrupt as life on the streets.

Britain had a profound role in the shaping of what India is today and therefore it is the British legacy of the Raj era which is being brought back to these shores. In theory therefore there is nothing to fear. Britain introduced so much: administration, judiciary, education, language, even religion. For all its faults, and Britain was not without fault, to a large extent it created much of Indian society. So you might think that a natural home from home for many Indians would be Britain.

The problem seems to be that while it was acceptable to introduce country clubs, tea parties and croquet to India and, in time, allow native Indians actually to join those clubs, it is quite another matter having Indians living next door to you back in 'Blighty'. One of two things happens in Britain when a family of one ethnic minority or another moves into the neighbourhood: either they are cold-shouldered and quickly find the frosty reception so unwelcoming that they leave, or the whites move out and in no time at all the area is transformed. Today less than 40% of the population in Newham, East London is white and it is the same in other parts of the country.

The author, Sanjay Suri, in his book *Brideless in Wembley*, describes driving up the M1 – 'Britain's Asian corridor' – to visit a friend in Leicester:

> *...I still always looked for excuses to take the M1 to Leicester. Maybe it's because so much of Leicester is Indian; it's the first big town in the West where whites are steadily declining into minority status. Partly because more Indians and other non-whites are coming in, growing and multiplying quite busily and partly because, seeing them, white people are leaving.*

Who are all these people so often dubbed simply 'Asians' or 'Pakis'? In fact they come from India, Pakistan, Bangladesh, Singapore, Burma, East Africa and Sri Lanka; racially they are all Indians in most respects. Pakistanis and Bangladeshis profess Islam whereas Indians have Hindu, Sikh, Muslim, Christian and Buddhist religions. The life of the people is, therefore, different in accordance with religion and other beliefs and habits including food, dress and language. There are people whose mother tongue is Punjabi, Urdu, Hindi, Gujarati, Bengali, Tamil etc., but most youngsters who are born and educated in this country speak English as their first language. With that confusing mix most of the problems facing Asian immigrant families can be related to these 'internal' factors which then run up against the outside influences of British culture

It is not that we are being swamped by immigrants but that those who come are congregating in single communities. No-one likes to see a crowd of youths of any colour walking along the street towards them. The same applies only more so when you have entire communities of one race or another. If, as a white English person, you get lost in your car and you accidentally wander off course into an 'ethnic' neighbourhood, you feel at best uneasy and at worst threatened. How many would simply stop the car, wind down the window and ask a group of lads the way? You feel that you might just as well throw your wallet out of the window.

Family and tradition are at the root of Indian society so at once we have a disconnection between Indians and the host nation. The British scarcely raise an eyebrow when someone divorces, for Indians it is a tragedy bringing shame on the family. While traditional ways may still hold in different parts of the country, the family unit is undoubtedly being challenged. There were more than 128,000 divorces in 2007 and in 2008/9 there were about 1.9 million single parent families in the UK, up by more than 238,000 since 1997. Although divorce rates are now said to be falling again this may only be because fewer couples are marrying in the first place. Asian parents are terrified by the divorce rate and the frightening increase in teenage pregnancies. Not so long ago the slogan aimed at teenagers was 'Smart girls carry condoms.' Now the latest advice from education pundits is targeted at eleven year old girls who are urged to carry condoms in their school bags.

Political parties argue constantly about the importance of the family; which one was pro-family and which was anti- as reflected in tax benefits. Personally I am pro the traditional family set up, but that is just one opinion. While the young face their challenges, those in the twilight of their life, particularly in the Asian community, feel lonely. If their sons and daughters choose to marry partners from the interracial and interreligious groups, the gap widens because of the vast cultural differences and family values. A great dilemma indeed. The

Western woman does not relish the close family ties. They feel threatened by the overpowering and loving relationship of her husband's family. On the other hand, parents feel left out, ignored and long for a closer family because traditional family patterns function on love and respect. Sympathy runs throughout the matrix of this living environment. The children learn within the family situation, while living harmoniously with parents and grandparents. Thus no one single person bears the strain of family life. The family is at one and at the same time a nursery for the young, support for the adult and a place of rest for the old. Age and wisdom along with love are the binding factors in the family.

Perhaps this sounds idealistic but it is the core philosophy of the family structure in the Asian community and it is a foundation of support not only for families but also for businesses which are usually inextricably linked to the family.

This disintegration of family life has devastated many in Asian society and, seeking solace for themselves, security and stability for their children, they turn to the scriptures. They came to the UK in search of a new life and better prospects and they ponder their *karma* about which Guru Nanak Dev, the founder of Sikhism says: *The string of roses is in the hands of Lord God. And man's own deeds drive him. Wherever his food is destined, he goes there to eat.* It sounds fatalistic to the outsider.

In India large extended families with grand and sometimes great grandparents, uncles, aunts and children of different generations living together is still a pattern with three-quarters of the population. Indians living in the UK want to replicate that pattern and it is causing problems, not only with the local white population, who view it all as rampant breeding little understanding the family structures, but also increasingly within the Indian families themselves.

Recently one mother wrote to me about the difficulties she was having persuading her fourth son to stay at home after his marriage along with his parents, three married brothers and their children. Rich and poor alike are committed to maintaining the name and fame of the family into posterity. There is an unbroken link between the past and the future and everyone is required to maintain the present. In India, families are a strength to society and to the nation.

By drawing attention to this, I should not be regarded as somehow anti-large family or indeed anti-extended family. Family life has its own pleasures that outweigh the pains. People learn to be honest, loving, caring, considerate and to help the needy members of the family. On the whole every member of the family strives to make the family unit happier, stronger and prosperous. This is the ideal Indian philosophy for a successful family life and there is no reason why the same should not apply to every family regardless of origin.

It is considered unpatriotic and even irreligious to break up the family but the sudden awakening to young men and women of other races can be as frightening as it is exciting.

One 16 year old girl wrote: *I am finishing my last year at school. The problem is that last year I went on a French exchange. I could not help but notice how good looking the foreign men were and was especially attracted to a young guy. We became good friends which then gradually led to close friends. There's no-one else I'd rather be with. He is coming to England to visit me, but my family do not know anything about this and would be horrified if they found out. I need to tell them quickly as they are arranging for me to view some young Asian men with the intention of getting me married once I've turned 18.*

Culture epitomises and represents a whole country; it is a way of life, its guiding light and the evolution of its civilisation. The conviction that Asian values are different, that the Asian ways of doing things are different and that the Asian attitude to say marriage is different, does not make it any easier either for the individual to accept them totally or, in this instance, for the host British population to accept them at all. It is crucial that all races understand each other's ways and that does not mean adopting one another's religions or customs, but it should mean appreciating, even celebrating the differences.

Because Asians are a minority group and because they felt that they were not accepted for what they were, the original immigrants tended to remain insular and avoided integration not only because of the hostility but also because of the desire to preserve their own identities and culture. I have received countless letters about the pressure often exerted on new generations not to assimilate with the host society, but to remain loyal to their parents' beliefs, culture and family ways. How often do young people write to me: *My boyfriend is my best friend. I love him …with strict parents like mine we don't see each other often.* The media and peer pressure imposed on this generation, which is at odds with these ethnic traditions, has caused intense misery in Asian families. It has led to young girls running away from home and their parents' constraints or inter-marrying with other races, disowning their own kind which in turn has caused cultural schizophrenia in the community. The multi-cultural and multi-racial conflict and confusion in the UK has been responsible for many divorces in the Asia community.

Izzat (honour of the family) has always been paramount for the Asian family. Parents have strived to protect their teenage daughters and sons from the glitter of the promiscuous Western society, which has resulted in double standards. Daughters abide by the parents' culture at home and then they try to be one of the herd when at school, university or place of work.

This is just one real life story which demonstrates what is happening today behind the often genteel façade.

Zeenat rebelled against her parents' warnings and constant lectures about making compromises with Western culture and about being submissive as the age-old traditional demands of the female members of their society. She quietly left home to live with her boyfriend. Her parents were furious and, with the help of private detectives, she was taken from her lover's home and brought back to her parents. In her anger, Zeenat informed the police about her abduction. Her father was arrested and still languishes in prison. Zeenat is now wracked by remorse and regret.

In the last twenty years, there has been tremendous change in the image of the Asian family. Earlier when Asians emigrated to Surinam, West Indies, America and Canada, their outlook on life, their mother tongue, culture and traditions remained almost intact for nearly thirty years. But then no-one had heard of Concorde, satellite, computers, mobiles and emails; that was the era when the entire village came with Puja flowers – marigold garlands –- to bid farewell to the person leaving. Parents were broken hearted and sobbed that they would never be able to see their sons again. Today the continents are as far apart as ever and yet the distances seem to have shrunk amazingly. In the last twenty years, the Asian community's values and outlook on life has also changed significantly.

But is this change good for the family or the individual? One correspondent complained: *I am suffering from acute depression. It started when my married daughter was sent back home by her husband and in-laws because she was distressed by her husband's English girlfriend. He returned home late in the evenings and spent weekends with her. My daughter was left at home to do all the housework for her mother-in-law. Then my son started living with his English girlfriend and refused to follow Asian marriage proposals. We did not know that another shock was around the corner for us. When my younger daughter ran away from home, I wish we had never come to this country. In our old age, you know, we feel like orphans.*

Teenage Indians, particularly girls, are caught in the multicultural maze. Life for second and third generation Indians in Britain feels like being trapped between two worlds. One is inhabited by their parents, who cling to their ethnic culture, family discipline, morality and religious roots in some sort of time warp, foisting on their children the value and norms they remember from their own formative years. The other world is infinitely more attractive. All you have to do is 'chill and take it easy' because there are no rules. It seems to embody the very essence of liberty and who in their right mind would reject it?

In this embarrassing and lonely situation they feel confused and consumed by the overpowering and colourful 'hip' Western culture. On the other hand, haunted by the parental and peer warning, fearful and unable to cope with the confusion, some run away from home. In desperation and torn between the love for her boyfriend and the family pressure to conform, one girl declared: *I don't care about the colour of his skin. I'm not bothered what people have to say, so I have decided to elope.* This is one of the most painful and terrifying situations. Tragically some girls think they have found true love but once away from home they are forced into prostitution and others are taken to the sub-continent under the pretext of getting married at home. Once there their passports are confiscated and the helpless, lonely girls are re-sold to the old, disabled or to pimps.

These fears and confusions strike young – one girl, just sixteen, asked me if I could help her run away from home because her father would not let he go out with her friends; another teenager was desperate to marry her Muslim boyfriend to escape the controlling ways of her father.

Religious influence often plays a significant part in holding back integration and creating rifts within the families. I will consider the role of religion more fully but some parents expect their daughters and daughters-in-law to be like Sita, the greatest symbol of purity, submission and faithfulness. Sita is a heroine of the Ramayan epic written in Sanskrit by the poet and sage, Valmiki, sometime in the period between 200 BC and 200 AD. It accentuates the sanctity of married love and the sacredness of a pledge. It is a living example of domestic and social values and deep faith in the ultimate meaning of life as a struggle between good and evil. Sita is generally viewed as the loyal wife of Lord Rama. For centuries Indian women have been taught to be faithful and subservient like Sita.

All the misconceptions about marriage and inter-marriage will be discussed in detail but for now we should just remember that it is important for the host country to look beyond the calm front often portrayed by Asian families and understand what tensions hide beneath the surface. In particular it should consider the younger generations who are naturally gregarious and would like to reach out but who feel tied to the traditional ways. These young people are the bridge but often they feel rejected and this is not a matter of wealth or education. I know sons of billionaires with degrees and great sophistication who state quite bluntly that real integration is simply not happening.

While many Asians live here, prosper and bring up their families, mentally some still long to be at home in India; they will always be in India, they prefer India and many may actually dislike Britain but they have no option other than to stay. To put it cynically the benefits and facilities far outweigh the pull of the land of their birth. In any case the reality is the link has long since been broken. There is no place for them back 'home'.

In fairness the same could be said for the Irish who came over in their thousands and set to work digging the streets. Even today, many decades on, an Irishman still rejoices in his Irish-ness, but then he is white and probably enjoys living here.

Is that essentially what it amounts to – the colour of one's skin? After all it cannot be the food Indians eat; curry is the new national dish of Britain. It is not the entertainment Indians enjoy as there is increasingly a cross-over between Hollywood and Bollywood; 'Bend It Like Beckham', the film about the struggle of an Indian girl striving to play football with all the culture clashes that involved, was a big hit in the UK, the sitar was made popular as far back as the Beatles era.

An interesting part of the Beckham film was how the young female star hid her football clothes in her bag and changed when she was away from home. This is commonplace among young Indian girls. While they are at home they follow the traditional code and styles but once beyond the reach of parental influence, they are quickly into their fashionable Western outfits which often leave little to the imagination. This dual existence is a constant source of upset in many Indian households.

What the girls are doing, however, is trying not to look different from their Western friends, in short they want to integrate and blend with their surroundings. They are behaving instinctively, an almost natural sense of self-preservation, a reaction from the wild, not to stand out and not to look different to avoid conflict.

By contrast many in the Arab world appear to go out of their way to look different. The women wear the *niqab* – full veil – we are told with pride, almost to say we are superior to you, we are more religious and more demure. They may be right even though there is nothing in Islam which insists on such a dress code, but the effect on the indigenous British population is to provoke anger. What if Britain were to pass a law forbidding the wearing of veils in this country as they have done in France? In Saudi Arabia, all women regardless of race or creed are obliged to cover the heads, wear long sleeves and are forbidden to wear revealing clothes. If it is good enough to pass such a law in Saudi Arabia, why not pass the opposite laws here?

Obviously this would not be done but the point is that traditional dress codes if worn 'aggressively', saying look at me I am different, succeed only in putting up barriers and preventing integration. I know many, particularly the younger women born and bred in the UK, would argue that they are not putting up barriers, rather they are expressing their individuality. But do they want to integrate? For most white British I would hazard a guess and say they find the n*iqab* off putting, probably offensive and even downright provocative in the current climate of fear over terrorism.

Covering your whole face in this manner prompts the question particularly for new arrivals: if everything about Western society is so deplorable why come here? The answer of course is that life in the UK is, by comparison, a bed of roses where there are no religious police, no such strict rules of conduct and freedom to indulge oneself perhaps as one cannot do at home, wherever that might be.

As we shall see in the pages about marriage, such hypocrisy is commonplace certainly in the Asian community and the thousands of letters I receive are testimony to such double standards. What they also show is that this community is gradually breaking apart, albeit very slowly. The new generation do not have the historical reference points of their parents and grandparents. They are not Indians, they are English. It may suit the boys to cling on to the old ways where they enjoy the freedom to play around while the girls remain faithful and true, but those double standards have been rumbled. Indian women have embraced the business freedoms on offer in the UK as well as the social freedoms. They are running their own businesses and are becoming millionaires in their own right.

For parents and grand-parents such a momentous change in traditional family life is often heart breaking and it is a sorrow suffered in silence behind closed doors to avoid the shame of what their neighbours might think.

So what will future British Indians enjoy? Will they pick and choose *à la carte* from both cultures? In a strange way this might be the beginning of true integration, choosing the best from both worlds. It does not mean the end of family life it just means the end of a narrowly focused family life, a life where there is one rule for the men and another for the women. This does not mean Women's Lib, which many might argue did nothing for women's rights, but a more equitable sharing of responsibilities as well as rewards.

Traditional Indian teaching urges people to work hard at your job, praise god and share your riches with others less fortunate than yourself. Such admirable sentiments can hardly be divisive between any races, indeed are probably common to most. So the focus must surely be on the commonalities of man. But to focus on those requires understanding and knowledge which, at its most basic, requires people to talk to each other. This is where the British are at fault and it will take many generations of integration to eradicate the legendary British reserve.

The white British cannot stand in the glasshouse throwing stones at their new fellow citizens if they resolutely fail to talk to them. Once upon a time the British were so interested in India that they ran the country, sending fleets thousands of miles round the Cape of Good Hope to build a massive infrastructure that stands today. It is a wonder that they ever left port. Perhaps it is one thing to be an intrepid explorer and conqueror in far off lands and quite another to live next door to 'one of those foreigners' in Acacia Avenue.

This then is both the reality and the dilemma facing Britain today. It is a country which forever more will be a mixture of different races, colours and creeds. The original indigenous population may well be white but there are already several generations of English born citizens who are not. This is their home. Britain has its own traditional values and it should be proud of them and resist changes to those traditions, particularly when they are attacked for being non-inclusive for people of a different origin. They are British traditions and if immigrants do not like them they should not seek to persuade some pusillanimous government to change them so that the country becomes all things to all men. It cannot be such a thing. If you prefer speaking French live in France, if you prefer to speak Urdu you can but do not expect to be given an interpreter at the tax payer's expense because you cannot be bothered to learn English.

On the other hand the British should accept that some people choose to dress differently, even worship in different styles and places. This is entirely acceptable so long as there is no attempt to coerce everyone else into believing what they believe and equally it does not transgress everyone's inalienable right to voice an opinion which might contradict those beliefs. We should be able to celebrate the diversity of the Britain with all its ethnic groups and yet be able to retain what has made Britain attractive to outsiders, most notably its freedom. Instead of worrying so much about the packaging maybe we should think more about the person within.

India is a secular society and all government and administration are run along secular lines but that does not prevent there being a diverse range of religions worshipping freely according to their customs. Other religions are more aggressive in their proselytising and the time may be overdue when such aggression is curtailed by the British authorities.

Everyone should be inquisitive about the world around them. Aristotle wrote: 'All men by nature desire to know.' (*Metaphysics*). Do not criticise or mock a man for wearing a turban but find out why he does so, what does it signify and what are its origins. Once we knew enough about curry we tucked into it like there was no tomorrow. We 'educated' ourselves about the different dishes and some fancy themselves as connoisseurs of a good curry. Why can we not explore other aspects of Indian culture and why can Indians not be more inquisitive about Britain? If you are invited into an Indian home you will always be offered an Indian meal, never English, Italian or French cuisine. We do not just eat roast beef.

In a word we must try to understand. That is the first essential step which has to begin in our families and then in the wider community. Both Indian and British culture has already changed and will continue to change. It is impossible to resist, but what is important is how we adapt to this process. We cannot run away from home like the frightened and frustrated teenager, we cannot weep into our tea behind closed doors and barred windows and we cannot force anyone to do anything against their will. In other words we must find a way to co-exist and that has to be by a process of education.

Chapter Two

Willingness to Learn

Never before has there been such great academic achievement in Britain. Never before have so many young people been attending university and colleges of further education; although it is debatable how many of the 362,015 granted student visas in 2009 – up 35% on the previous year – were planning to attend *bone fide* courses. But even if we give them all the benefit of the doubt, never before has the population with its myriad ethic communities and all its learning understood so little about each other.

Education should be the opportunity for people from all races finally to achieve an equal footing on the ladder of life particularly in a country like England – and I'll focus here on England as that is where most immigrants settle. There is so much on offer: free education, free school meals.

The reality, of course, is different. Indian and Chinese students are more likely to achieve their targets than other ethnic groups, notably Black, Pakistani and Bangladeshi pupils. A study by the Department of Education and Skills in collaboration with the University of Birmingham showed that while socio-economic factors of individual families are significant, there is still a difference in performance along ethnic lines.

Education is regarded as a key priority among the educated Indian classes – 85 per cent of students stay on to complete further education. There is no question that Indian children as a group are hard workers and high achievers. There is pressure for them to succeed and get the best qualifications. Good results lead to good jobs and economic prosperity. Parents will continuously goad their children on to work harder, get better marks and above all achieve a professional qualification. And yet that is not the whole picture.

It is important always to remember that there is one rule for boys and one rule for girls in Indian society regardless of status in life. The only real difference between rich and poor is the harshness of life for girls from poorer families and the different pressures.

At the bottom end of the economic ladder there are letters from girls whose parents – usually fathers – are simply following the letter of the law by reluctantly agreeing for their daughters to go to school.

One wrote: *I don't think I've ever seen eye to eye with my father since I was 14 or so. That was when I went to school because by law I had to. After my GCSEs, that was it. Education would give me ideas that I didn't need. My future was to be a suitable wife. All that was needed was good cooking and cleaning skills.*

At the other end of the social spectrum every child regardless of sex is encouraged, even pushed, to work hard, do their studies and their homework and if possible to achieve a good degree. But when it comes to university life you can almost hear the crashing of gears as suddenly the daughter, who was safely under the protection of her family, returning home every day, is now thrown into a bewildering world of halls of residence, parties and boys.

The terrible strain for one family taking their daughter to university in Manchester for the first time was obvious. Their daughter had never spent a night away from home and suddenly she was to be 'released' into the jungle of university life. In the girl's eyes you could read a mixture of fear and anticipation.

Such a clash of cultures inevitably throws up a whole raft of psychological problems. For the student there is the battle between probably a strict upbringing, where adherence to traditions and faith played a strong part at home, and the free-for-all of student life where every belief is challenged and anything goes. For the first time there is no-one to say no. There is no-one to force you to attend lectures or do your studies. There is no-one to criticise if you return to your digs drunk with a boy or girl on your arm.

For the parents there is the fear of what might be happening to their little girl and even concern about what their little boy might be up to. Is he being led astray by the ill-disciplined 'goras' (whites) and is he doing his studies? Even if their children are conscientious and pass their exams well, there is a fear of losing them to the outside world. There is always an underlying tension in the family that the very gift of education might become the cause of a split. The son of a shop-keeper or bus driver might easily become a doctor or a lawyer. He will inevitably move away from his family socially which leaves parents bereft or worse abandoned; how often do we hear about children who have become 'middle class' and instead of following the tradition of looking after their parents under the same roof, put them in care homes for the elderly. This is the anguish and the penalty that some parents have to face as their children move ahead.

But before university there is the schooling process to get through and as society has become segregated and polarised into different ethnic groups, so too has education. And yet schooling is not just about education, it is also about social integration – learning how to get on with your fellow man. If everyone in the catchment area is of Asian origin it is inevitable that most of the children will be Asian. That has its benefits in one sense because there is less bullying based on ethnic background; young Sikh boys are not teased because of the way they wear their hair. But such isolation teaches children nothing about learning to live with people from a different social and ethnic background.

Where schools are truly mixed children face daily the psychological problem of living a double existence, a dual life –

English or Western style by day and Indian by night. They do not want to be seen to be different and actually want to be regarded as English, although they are every inch an Indian. But the emphasis is on style or rather appearance; they will wear western clothes, party like Westerners, drink like Westerners, but that should not be confused with being integrated. They remain in their own groups. Nevertheless, most children probably do not even give it a second thought; they are used to the double life and may not even be conscious of it. Issues only arise if, when it is time to get married, their son or daughter has decided against the odds that they would like to marry someone who is not Indian. In such situations, it is the parents who have the biggest hurdle to cross. But this is not unique to Indians; white British parents would also have long, worried discussions between themselves late into the night if one of their children suddenly announced that they were marrying an Indian.

Typically English schools follow the standard curriculum. Where religion is taught it is usually to raise awareness of other faiths as an intellectual exercise. It is only in some of the Muslim schools where the Koran and its teachings dominate everyday life. The effect of this type of education seems to accentuate the differences between the children and their host nation.

Faith schools *per se* are not a problem but it is important that they should be a part of the overall educational system and not separate from it. In 2007 there were seven state-funded Muslim schools compared with over 4,700 Church of England schools, 2,100 Catholic schools, 37 Jewish and 28 Methodist schools. The danger is encouraging faith schools to stand alone and actively promote themselves as different and, worse, somehow superior. That road leads to deeper division and not integration.

The Commission for Racial Equality (CRE) warned in the past that the UK was *'sleep walking into racial segregation'* and that the country's increasingly segregated schools were *'school-*

ing people to be strangers to each other'. The comments sparked an outcry but they at least drew attention to what my correspondents have already noted: the much vaunted multi-cultural society in fact ends at the school gates.

There could have been no more obvious case of non-conforming than the Muslim teaching assistant who wanted to wear a full veil at work. In the end she lost her appeal. An employment tribunal ruled that she had not been discriminated against when her school suspended then sacked her after staff at the Church of England school where she was teaching said they had had complaints from pupils that they could not understand what she was saying. It is interesting to note the different attitude between a Sikh family who will accept that their son can cut his hair so as not to stand out from the rest and the attitude of some Muslims who wish to look so distinctive. The argument for wearing a particular uniform at school is precisely so children can have a sense of belonging and also so that there is none of the one-upmanship about what particular brand of jeans or sneakers one is wearing; that in itself can lead to bullying and put unwelcome pressure on parents to keep up with the Joneses.

The real concern must surely be that as different sections of the community fall behind others, the economic gap will increase. Gradually people will move away from the poorer neighbourhoods if they can and those that cannot will be left behind. If the standard of achievement in a school is generally low then it follows that the students will be unable to break out of their increasingly impoverished communities and the overall decline accelerates. But what is noticeable is that the upwardly mobile Indian families tend to move to areas where other successful families have established a 'bridgehead' – so the old impoverished ghetto has been replaced with one which is mink-lined.

A report back in 2007 by the Joseph Rowntree Foundation, the UK's largest independent social policy research and development charity, called for *'an urgent rethink from government and employers, so that minority ethnic groups do not miss out on opportunities in the workplace and higher educational attainment is properly recognised.'*

Foundation Director, Julia Unwin, said, *'Even with a degree, Pakistani and Bangladeshi men are less likely to be employed than someone white with the same qualifications. Despite a rapid growth in Pakistani and Bangladeshi women going to university, they suffer high unemployment and are much less likely than Indian or white British women to be in professional, or managerial, jobs.'*

I wonder what if anything has really changed in the intervening years.

The question for educationalists is what can they do to assist the process of integration; indeed should it be up to schools? Is it up to government or to parents? Teachers have to tread carefully. Even if they had enough time in their day to explore new ways of integration, the reality is they are just struggling to get through the timetable, faced with classes where English is not the first language. There is little parents can do because they are already trapped in a world which does not encourage mixing with people outside the neighbourhood.

So what can governments do? Yes, they can insist on faith schools falling into line with state education, they can legislate about school uniforms but they are faced with a multiplicity of cultures, of people who do not know how to communicate with each other at the most basic level of a common language. The other alternative is to engineer artificially a change of mix in schools. The CRE suggested looking at a change in catchment areas for schools but that smacks of US–style bussing of children from one neighbourhood to another. One experiment is to create new multi-faith academies as part of a plan to combat racial segregation bringing different ethnic groups together – but does this amount to social engineering as some have claimed?

The truth of the matter is you cannot force people to mix if they do not want to. Blackburn with Darwen Council had to admit that there was no guarantee that a £150 million initiative to transform education and bring higher levels of integration would work. They wanted to create three 'super-schools' which would bring the borough's four faith schools together and broaden their intake. Critics of the scheme said parents would send their children to schools of their own faith. The local newspaper, the *Lancashire Telegraph*, conducted a poll and asked if people thought the plans would improve integration – 80% disagreed.

What is the logical consequence of not doing anything – possibly even sharper dividing lines between the ethnic groups and in universities, traditional hotbeds of radical thought and the encouragement of extreme ideas? Universities, for now at least, are probably the most integrated communities in the country. A wonderful United Nations of learning where you have no say and no idea whom you will be sitting next to in a lecture hall or living next to in halls of residence. For three or four years it seems everyone's natural innate prejudices are dropped as students have the common aim of having fun and passing their degrees. Probably for the only time in their lives hundreds of different racial groups have a unified purpose.

Why do these same students all suddenly revert to type at the end of it all? The answers are probably both prosaic and cultural. The need to get out and earn a living is uppermost in most students' minds having built up sizeable debts. Throughout university they have had few responsibilities and not been concerned about the harsh realities of life. Students who were good friends at college or university gravitate back to their own neighbourhoods and drift apart. The great prize would be to capture and nurture that friendship when it exists to ensure it survives into later life.

For the Indian students their obligations to family kick in with a responsibility to support the family as well as getting married. I will discuss marriage in a later chapter but this institution alone is a major division. This is a delicate time when splits can occur and the older generation are clear where the blame lies. One father wrote to me saying: *I am fifty-two. Have six children. Only the two younger ones are at home. The older four, we don't see them. We don't know where they are. Got married to Goras or just disappeared. I have been suffering from acute depression...I am tired of this miserable life.*

Another Asian father, typical of so many, also blamed the 'corrupting' effect of whites. He could not tolerate his young, beautiful daughter's decision to marry a man from a different culture and religion. When he heard the news, he was rushed to hospital suffering from a stroke. He had to retire from his job aged forty.

What chance is there for 'community cohesion' when people of different races in their very hearts and being think and behave differently? What chance is there for inter-community understanding when there is no common language and even a wilful refusal to learn English? You can pass laws saying women and men are equal, but that counts for nothing behind closed, even locked, doors. One distressed wife called to say that she was locked in her house every day by her husband when he left for work because he was convinced she would have an affair if she went out.

We are living in an age of rapid discovery, new facts of life, nature and beliefs; there are new inter-relationships, inter-dependences and interactions among peoples from around the world. For both student and teacher, the present offers an exciting opportunity while well-established facts are suddenly obsolete and old-school.

In moments of transformation, metamorphosis and reconstruction, some institutions and structures crumble and, as if from nowhere, a new panorama of delight takes their place. People have to adapt and readjust not only in physical terms, but also mentally. Some change can be unpleasant, even painful, but it is time for a new beginning.

Family, parents and children constitute one such institution which is undergoing change particularly in urban society. The UK and particularly England is a densely populated island that is experiencing enormous turmoil and, as ever, it is children who bear the brunt but also have the greatest opportunity. Nevertheless change at the present time is probably too rapid and too complex for families to comprehend.

Revolutionary changes are taking place. Britain, whether its indigenous population likes it or not, is a multicultural, multi-racial and multi-faith society. From the moment the doors were thrown open in the sixties there was no going back. Schools are at the forefront of those changes; the new educational pattern has to accommodate religious, psychosocial and cultural peculiarities of the thousands of new immigrants who arrive on its shores every single day. The newcomers bring with them different ideas and mores, for them culture, marriage and society mean different things from their new host society. The only certainty is that this potentially dangerous mix can only be handled with that great British attribute, compromise. It is an attribute immigrants to these islands will have to learn along with the language; it is not sufficient for the British to be the ones bending to the whims and habits of the newcomers unless of course Britain itself is prepared to be changed forever.

Britain does have a history of change and assimilation and to that extent the schools can teach at least that similarity with India. You cannot stop a nation developing; if history is a continuous movement of people in time, it is also a continuous transmission of the past into the texture of the present and the future. It is indeed an unbroken process of assimilation giving rise to a new culture through a constant interchange and interplay. What is known as the Indian Culture today is in reality a rich mosaic which has developed through the ages. India's immense diversity baffles at times. Many foreigners wonder how a people, so diverse racially, physically, linguistically and religiously can call itself a nation and above all, hold together as a nation. Its diversity is an historical legacy which strengthens its national fabric instead of weakening it. Unity in diversity has been the guiding force behind India's evolution. That is a lesson Britain can learn if, as it does, it feels threatened by its visitors. Its diversity should be seen as a gift, an opportunity to move still further ahead. So when schools come to study the ethnic mix of the British people, instead of picking up a black and a white doll and saying these are the differences, as was done in the past, they can celebrate the strides the UK has made in science, industry, finance thanks to the extraordinary kaleidoscope of world knowledge it has absorbed.

The onus therefore to a certain extent is on schools because that is where young people spend most of their formative years and it is also the one place where children in segregated communities can at least have the opportunity of mixing with other races. Sadly, it is a slim hope, particularly when one realises that increasingly schools themselves are becoming single or predominantly single race.

For Indian parents there is an equally strong challenge: to learn to let go. Sons and daughters living, learning and loving in the Western world, cannot keep their eyes shut. In reality they are the lucky ones, they have the support and security of the family home and yet have the opportunity to learn more than the parents could ever have done. They are mixing with fellow students at university from literally around the globe and should seize the chance to learn from them.

Government's responsibility must be to create the climate for learning, rooting out extreme views and divisive teaching and insisting that all teaching establishments are there for the benefit of the students and not to promote some cause. The other problem for governments to address is racism not only among children but against teaching staff as well. According to the Institute for Policy Studies in Education black teachers in particular suffer racial abuse on a daily basis in the classroom. Their research indicated that black people form a very small minority of the teaching population also face discrimination from their colleagues. The study in London schools was undertaken in response to the need to recruit more teachers from minority ethnic communities. More than one third of London pupils come from minority ethnic communities.

In a separate study, the University of Brighton found Britain's education system to be 'institutionally racist' with pupils and teachers from ethnic minorities vulnerable to abuse. Other investigations into racism in schools in south-east England compiled by the University of Sussex, Canterbury Christ Church University College as well as the University of Brighton, concluded that *'covert racism exists almost everywhere'*.

Sometimes the underlying problem is simply one of discipline. Pupils are allowed to get away with comments without being reprimanded. One Asian teacher resigned from his primary school because there were so many rules and regulations not only preventing disciplinary measures but also the political correctness which did not allow him to treat children like children, comforting them when they were upset by holding them or picking them up when they fell in the playground for fear of accusations of abuse.

Despite the obvious heartache retold in countless letters I have received suffered by many parents and children pulled apart by conflicting cultures, Indian families are unlikely to reject the opportunities the British education system has to offer. The focus is one hundred per cent on achieving high qualifications despite the obstacles in the way. If there is trouble at the school, the advice would be to keep your head down, avoid conflict and focus on your studies. Nine times out of ten that formula works but it does not make for lasting friendships across the racial divide. The education system in the UK does reward hard workers and high achievers and, as night follows day, that simply alienates those clearly identifiable groups who fail in their academic studies. Teachers like to work with conscientious pupils and gravitate to the best schools. There is a selection process in all schools simply by virtue of their location – to put it bluntly as the neighbourhood deteriorates so does the rest of the fabric of the area and that includes schools who find it hard to attract quality staff. To be tough is to be 'cool' and 'tough guys' don't bother with homework.

Consider the experience of the Indian community in the UK since the sixties and seventies. Couples both worked hard throughout the week to earn money and save for the deposit on a house or start their own small business. Those were ambitious years. Full of hope. A bright future. For many that resulted in success with comfortable even affluent living standards and well-educated children. But not for one moment did the host community seek to integrate with these newcomers or invite them in for tea; in fact if they did not drive them out, the whites left the neighbourhood themselves because it had 'gone downhill.' So the Indian community drew themselves together and established a parallel and largely successful universe. Other immigrants did much the same, experienced much the same, but not all were as successful; nevertheless they established their own worlds. Now, well into the new millennium, we are trying to find ways to integrate these groups and make them 'British'. It is too late for such social engineering. The focus for educationalists, for this is where the groundwork must begin, is to help young people understand the different cultures around them and welcome the diversity as an opportunity to broaden their horizons.

Opening your mind is what education is all about but the big breakthrough will only happen when everyone truly opens their mind to the reality that we are all in the same boat. We have one life and the best way to get through it in harmony with our fellow citizens does not depend on the number of books we read or the colleges and universities we attend, it depends on our own individual attitudes to one another. If for just one moment in the day we can put ourselves second and our neighbour first, we will be taking a giant leap forward. All the letters and telephone calls I receive have one thing in common – someone's selfishness whether emotional, financial or sexual has upset another person; take the ego out of the equation and the core of any problem evaporates.

There is one last point about education – you are never too old to learn. I say this because students in schools, colleges and universities are continuously under pressure to perform. I have even urged them to lead the way in finding opportunities to integrate but at the other end of the scale people should not be surprised to find woeful ignorance among supposedly educated and sophisticated people – even those leading the country in the Houses of Parliament – about the citizens they claim to represent. Not out of malice, but possibly out of laziness or even genuine interest, they often display a stunning ineptitude in grasping the basic differences between the races and religions which, forever more, will make up the British family. This is not the place to explain the religious and ethic distinctions of all the peoples in the UK but ask many people about Asians or ask many Asians about the British and you will often find blank faces or misconceptions. I was listening to the radio recently and some English people were being asked the surname of the Royal Family – one suggested it might be Rex and only one remembered Windsor. There is clearly some way to go before our general knowledge encompasses our visitors if matters so close to home remain vague.

Chapter Three

Letting go of the old ways

Letting go is a hard lesson to learn. If you take up parachuting there comes a moment when you have to let go of the supporting struts on the plane for the first time and trust yourself, your life, to the parachute and the training you have received. When you are a small child you have to go into free-fall when you must let go of your mother's hand and walk bravely into school alone to face the unknown. At every stage of life we have to learn to let go; we finally earn our wings and fly solo. But do we? It is apparent from the correspondence and communications I receive that no-one really wants to let go, least of all of ourselves and our hang-ups.

Marriage is a time when we should be letting go of the apron strings tying us to our parents – usually our mothers – but so often those invisible umbilical chords are unbreakable. Letting go does not mean losing touch but it does mean growing up which in turn should mean growing in awareness and knowledge, but so often it means nothing of the sort. Asian parents are very possessive. They like to keep control of their children – girls and boys. As regards daughters, after their marriage the control passes to the in-laws and her husband and they in turn continue this with their own sons and daughters.

Marriage is the beginning of a family and a happy marriage has the traditional family values. But marriage is no longer considered to be made in heaven. This ancient institution has received such a battering in recent years that young people today have begun to find solace in the anonymous saying that *'marriage is an attempt to turn a night owl into a homing pigeon.'* When one in three marriages ends in divorce and three out of three are struggling with their marriage, what is the fate of the family?

The old song went *'Love and marriage, go together like a horse and carriage.'* Now few believe in those words. But marriage based on love lasts forever, until death do us part; eastern people, believing in the afterlife, never part. If they do, they part to meet again. This is the law of Wishful Karma to some. In the Vedic style, the bride at the marriage ceremony is blessed with the words: 'Be the queen to thy father-in-law, a queen to thy mother-in-law and for a life long and conjugal unity.'

With sons and daughters by their side
May the two enjoy the full span of life
Both decorated with ornaments of gold (R.VIII. 31-8)

So how does this help integration? A happy, united family is the basis of social unity among people of the world. Not everyone can make their life work. In your forties you begin to know how it is likely to 'pan out'. It is the same with marriages – you have to work at them if you want them to last.

Consider the differences. In the UK, the marriage scene is distinct in almost every respect. Sons-in-law and daughters-in-law call their mothers-in-law by their first names. All the sisters and brothers are addressed by their names and the same for uncles and aunts. Whereas for Asian families there is more formal respect for the extended family, each one with their own name: mother's sisters are all called *masiji* and brothers are *mamaji*. No-one would dream of calling any older person by name.

The second generation Asian immigrant is far less westernised than is generally realised by 'outsiders'. His westernisation does not generally extend beyond his mannerisms, language, dress, food habits or style of life. It rarely penetrates his innermost or primary identity which is essentially Asian. He remains rooted in his parental culture and imbibes only as much of the British way of life as is necessary to help him get by in British society without appearing odd or awkward.

The Asian family is extremely close-knit and characterised by considerable emotional inter-dependence. It is almost like a living organism whose members constitute its inter-dependent limbs. They share in common their triumphs and tragedies, joys and sorrows and depend on each other for guidance, encouragement and inspiration. As a result the young grow up lacking an exclusive notion of self and are unable to exist outside the supportive relationship of the family. They may intellectually subscribe to Western values but their emotional being is almost utterly un-Western. This diminishes their capacity to rebel and if they do rebel, the rebellion is largely symbolic.

Having said that, the clash of cultures can cause grave difficulty and bewilderment among the older Asian population; they have suffered because their children, especially the boys, no longer wish to look after their elderly parents in the traditional extended family structure living under one roof. These married and even unmarried boys copy the majority of the community and do not want the burden of looking after their parents. They go to the Gurdwara (temples), listen to the divine music, have their lunch or dinner at the temple in the traditional way, sitting with other people and discuss family problems but their saintly thoughts end there.

Then there is the family structure torn apart by the desire of the husband who wishes to return home to India unable to let go of his past life. There have been tragic stories of mothers refusing to uproot themselves to travel to a land they no longer know; some may have never lived in India. In desperation they have taken their children to the railway station and jumped in front of the oncoming trains. Such stories stunned family and community alike. The public could not understand what had happened to young families that would have driven them to such a breakdown, but the desperation is frightening in some families.

The question is: are the rest of us so different? What actually is happening is couples – not always just husbands – are unable to let go of their single lives; infidelity is often the root cause. One young bride who had been married within four weeks of arriving in the UK wrote in despair about her husband: *He started to spend the weekends away from home and if he came into the room he wouldn't speak to me. I could not bear this any more an asked him to tell me if he has someone else in his life. He admitted unhesitatingly and said: 'I did not want to marry you – it was your aunt who forced my mother, that after marrying a Punjabi girl I would give up the company of my English girlfriend – I love her very much and we have a year-old baby. You can go back to your aunt because I did not want to marry you in the first place.'*

Another girl cried bitterly about her husband's infidelity again complaining that he spent weekends away with another woman. She said she had been brought up to be a god-fearing daughter and straightforward girl. Her mother had warned her about the pitfalls of married life; be honest, co-operate with her husband, listen to him, don't shout and don't giggle like a girl, be careful and respectful towards the in-laws. Above all she was warned not to speak to the outside world about what happened in the home or the treatment she was getting. There was a long list of dos and don'ts. She took her own life.

One should not confuse taking a white mistress as a sign that socialising between white and Asian is happening – it is more a case of enjoying 'the forbidden fruits.' It is something for men to brag about among themselves, like a large, new car. They are still every inch Asian in their real world of business and family life.

Although Indian society even in the UK is for the most part a man's world, it is worth pointing out that some have managed to let go of old inhibitions in a startling way and increasingly female correspondents have revealed that for them life outside India is infinitely more appealing. One wrote with frank honesty to say: *I have a problem. I had an affair before I was married and we used to make love. Now I have been married for seven years but still enjoy sex with other men. I enjoy drinking and the company of men. I must have sex every day.* Her letter continued in the same vein even explaining that her husband was equally adventurous. While not condoning such actions, it is worth remembering that 80% of the Indian population lives in villages and most families live under one roof all their lives, this does not provide much privacy for couples to enjoy each other's company. When Asians first started coming to the UK in the sixties, many correspondents wrote asking some very basic questions about love making. One said: *Now that we have an independent home and complete privacy it is not like our village home where we were surrounded by other family members and we could not enjoy the sexual act.*

The conflict of arranged marriages and interracial relations are explored in more detail elsewhere but the issue here combines the very real day to day tensions facing the Asian community unable to manage their dual existence. Men enjoy the new freedom of the Western lifestyle while paying lip-service to Asian culture, while most women seem trapped in a half-way house, unable to 'benefit' from the libertarian mores of the West and yet too far removed from the now alien world of India.

With so many internal personal struggles going on in the Asian-British world it is difficult for outsiders to understand even the most basic issues Asians face in their daily lives. How can their hosts in the UK find a way into this world? In truth they cannot; the mixing when it happens is on a superficial level at the occasional party, at work or almost accidentally at a club. The mistake is trying to be too English or too Indian. It surely does not matter what the individual is. What we must try and do is truly to let go, not of our traditions, but of our hang-ups about each other. It does not matter where I worship or whether I worship at all, it does not matter how I dress or what I eat, in fact, if we can start by saying 'I' do not matter, but I am interested in 'you' then we will have made real progress. This is a tall order for all of us but it can work. One correspondent had written in desperation after suffering *'merciless beatings'* from her husband who had falsely accused her of having affairs, but she had managed to diffuse the situation: *I never said a harsh word to him or went out to the cinema or visited friends which I used to do as a revenge. So the beatings stopped, but he still suspects me of having affairs. I do not argue with him anymore but look after his needs, cook, clean and carry on my duties. He must realise that I am not what he likes to call me. I am a home loving and contented person and I will not have him accuse me without reason...He is finally coming round gradually.*

This is nothing short of heroic selflessness and difficult to comprehend in a world where we usually put ourselves first, but it is proof that putting ourselves second, without expectation of reward, can also bring happiness. Of course, the finest example of meeting violence with non-violence in modern history was Mahatma Gandhi himself, who vowed to lead India to freedom without firing a single shot. He was also the prime example of letting go of everything material. They say that when he died his total worldly possessions were worth two dollars.

Indians are deeply rooted in their traditions. The image of Sita – one of suffering, sacrifice, forbearance – as depicted in the Ramayan epic mentioned earlier, is typical. The word 'sita' means furrow, the line made by the plough. It also happens to be the name of the goddess associated with ploughed fields in Vedic literature. She represents the fertility of the ploughed earth and the necessity of a male power to awaken, arouse and inseminate the earth. In the legend she is literally 'unearthed' by her father ploughing the fields. For Indians having lived in the UK for many years, made money and enjoying the riches of success – large house, large car, flourishing business, a son and a daughter and plenty of staff – they remain remote from the host community. While the second and third generations may speak English as a first language and say Punjabi as a second language, they still keep themselves to themselves. Although the Spanish artist, Picasso lived and worked in France he used to say that no matter where a man lives, he always belongs to his native village. In the same way so many Asians make the annual pilgrimage home renewing and reawakening family memories and traditions.

Despite living here for 40 years or more, parents still interfere with their children's lives; they will never say 'O, it's their life, let them carry on the way that suits them.' They refuse to let go. This is the main reason why parents do not like their sons to marry English girls who are seen as too independent. Unlike the Indian bride who often becomes totally subservient to her new mother-in-law, and in the worst cases simply just another of her servants, the young English girl will have her own ideas and want to lead her own life entirely separate from her in-laws and certainly not under the same roof. Asian parents want to know what their children are doing at all times. They go on pumping them with the traditions, culture and language of their ancestry and the lecturing goes on even after marriage because it is an interlinked, interwoven and inter-dependent society.

The conviction that Asian values are different, coupled with the feeling that they are not even accepted for what they are, makes many Asians believe that they are constantly being subjected to social pressures and therefore why bother to integrate; instead they seek to preserve their own identities and culture and why not as, from a purely commercial and financial point of view, it is clearly working?

So far we have focussed on the difficulties of the Indian families who, some might say, are stuck in their old ways unlike the British who are modern and free of all the baggage of ... Well the baggage of what – tradition, culture, respect, obedience? The

British have all these things. But are they really such a heavy burden? They are if we see them as a load to carry. But if we preserve the best of traditions, culture and respect in order to help our neighbours rather than to build up barriers to keep them out, then they become building blocks to unity.

No-one has to be a learned scholar to realise that by helping someone they are far more likely to offer you assistance in return than to throw a brick through your window; the point is though you are actually doing something. Gandhi's campaign of non-violence was not a campaign of inaction. In the same way it is just as bad to ignore your neighbour as to be rude to him. You cannot sit at home, the curtain twitching, wishing your neighbour would actually sell up and go and at the same time tell yourself you have never done him any harm. Sigmund Freud said that *'thought is action in rehearsal.'* Eknath Easwaran, the scholar who established his Blue Mountain Center for Meditation in California, said in his book, *The End of Sorrow*, *'When we are thinking angry thoughts against somebody, we are actually throwing abstract rocks.'*

The British, like every other race, has to slough off the protective skin they use to keep their guests away. Speaking from personal experience, my husband and I, like many of the earliest immigrants to the UK, received much help and support from our neighbours, but it was always 'at arm's length' as though they would somehow be diminished by too close an association.

In order to break down this barrier a need has to be created – nobody does anything for nothing, although it is an aspiration for which we should all strive. That need is all around us and that need is to recognise that all human beings are inter-dependent; you cannot do anything to one person without having an immediate reaction against someone else – even if that person is yourself; plus and minus, positive and negative, ying and yang.

The reality is that we are all very alike with the same hangups, worries, hopes and dreams as each other regardless of background. The focus should be less on the packaging and more on the content or, as the old saying goes, don't judge a book by its cover.

Just as the novice parachutist had to release his grip to enjoy the exhilaration of floating through the air, so do we all have to let go of our fears and inhibitions to enjoy the experience of freefall through the diversity around us. To extend the metaphor a little, if we hang on to all our baggage of prejudices and assumptions when we jump we will hurtle to the ground, but if we are free from such inhibitions, and that includes being free from thinking only of ourselves, then we will enjoy the 'flight'. Those who meditate experience the same moment of release when they are able to let go of the clutter of life for a time.

It goes entirely against the grain of human nature to drop one's defences so totally that one is no longer 'in control'. So long as the parachute holds we are safe but we find it hard to believe until we actually jump from the plane and look up at the billowing silk above our head. The same is true if we try to conduct ourselves without first thinking of 'what's in it for me?' What will the new neighbours be like? Will I like them? Will they cook smelly food? Will they have rowdy parties? The mother-in-law to be also has so many worries: who will my son marry, will she be good enough, will she be a loving wife and daughter-in-law, will she obey or will she rebel? The bride is equally concerned, particularly if she has only recently got to know the bridegroom's family and perhaps even the bridegroom himself: will they be kind, will he be faithful and the list goes on. The solution to all these worries and, in fact with every worry, is to shift the focus from your worries to their worries – how can I be welcoming to my new neighbour, how can I make the young nervous bride relax, how can I be even more loving to my spouse? Instantly the pressure is off because the focus has shifted from 'me' to 'you'.

The terrible flaw reflected in the title of this book is that in fact we do all need each other and depend utterly on each other. Think of it as a traffic question; if I drive a big car there is less room for my neighbour to drive his car; if I consume more oil and petrol, then I am consuming more fossil fuels quite apart from polluting the atmosphere which is making it harder for the world to breathe. We do very much need each other. When we are ill we need to have the doctors and nurses to attend to us but if they cannot find somewhere to live locally how will they be able to reach the hospital? Letting go does not mean disregarding the rest of the community in which we live, it means recognising that we are utterly dependent on each other and every living creature. It means letting go of our arrogance of supposed self-sufficiency and accepting the words of John Donne that we are not alone: *All mankind is of one author, and is one volume; when one man dies, one chapter is not torn out of the book, but translated into a better language; and every chapter must be so translated...As therefore the bell that rings to a sermon, calls not upon the preacher only, but upon the congregation to come: so this bell calls us all: but how much more me, who am brought so near the door by this sickness.... No man is an island, entire of itself...any man's death diminishes me, because I am involved in mankind; and therefore never send to know for whom the bell tolls; it tolls for thee.*

Chapter Four

Let's party ... alone

If man is a social animal – Indians have turned it into an art form; impromptu gatherings for a simple meal or a chat are far more likely than the English equivalent of putting something in the diary two weeks hence. Nevertheless while both groups like to party they choose to party alone.

Whose fault is that? The only honest answer is that both are to blame; when our first approach to introduce ourselves to our new neighbours is rebuffed we do not try again. 'Well let them get on with it,' we say, 'to hell with them.' The mistake, of course, is taking no for an answer. We should go on handing out the invitations and go on giving a cheery wave until the frost begins to thaw; easier said than done but that must be the right approach because the alternative only leads to the growing resentment and hostility we see around us today.

It was not always like this. When the very first Asians came to Britain in the late forties and fifties there was curiosity to begin with; the flowing saris and exotic looking turbans probably brought a welcome splash of colour to the drab, post-war streets when rationing was still in force. Asians were not invited in to British homes, of course, but there was no outright racism – that was to follow. Landladies did turn Asians away when they knocked on the door looking for lodgings, but in a way that was understandable; they were confronted by a strange, coloured face and in any case accommodation was scarce.

In London there were only a handful of Indian restaurants but it was possible to get a plate of chicken curry and dahl with paranthas for a few shillings. Despite the hardships Asians always managed to gather to cook and eat together at weekends for lunch or dinner and dancing *bhangra*. New arrivals from 'home' always brought supplies such as rice, papadums, chutney and pickles which went a long way; rice was in such short supply at the time that families often made do with crushed vermicelli as a substitute. In one sense those were happy-go-lucky times even though everyone was serious about their chosen work. That was the time women encouraged their sons and daughters take their O Levels (GCSEs) then leave school and start earning for the family as soon as possible. In those days some mothers would write to complain if their son had decided instead to prolong his education by going to university. That attitude was to change.

Soon, however, divisions started appearing. Initially after Indian Independence the first Indian arrivals in the UK probably had no intention of settling permanently in the country; the dream was always to return home and even now, in late middle age, even old age, for some that dream persists. Later on into the late fifties and early sixties as word filtered back home of the new land of plenty, large groups would arrive looking for long term, even permanent, work. In those days 'established' Asians acted as guides to those considering travelling to the UK; they advised men to list large numbers of 'children' on their passports, even if they were not their own, so that when they arrived in the UK they could claim benefits. And, of course, those same guides were on hand to explain how the applications for welfare should be made as many of the arrivals could not speak a word of English.

At that stage still most were Punjabi Sikhs, Hindus and Muslims from both India and Pakistan and came from a rural background. Instinctively recognising the obstacles ahead they were happy to go for factory jobs where shift work would allow them to earn good money despite the fact that many of them had university degrees and higher education qualifications. By comparison to the few rupees they earned at home even in 'senior' positions, they felt wealthy indeed and were able to send funds back to support the families they had left behind. One of the great boasts at the time as men gathered in pubs to compare payslips was that they were earning more than the Indian Prime Minister! It was not long however before problems arose with the native population as they moved into local accommodation near the factory workplace. The offensive smell of curry was high on the list of complaints.

There were soon small inroads into the social fabric though: flower power coupled with yoga, the Maharishis and the Beatles became all the rage. Then the sitar and musicians like Ravi Shankar began to influence western music – again the Beatles set the trend. Television picked up the Indian theme and productions like 'Gandhi' and 'Jewel in the Crown' raised the profile. Thus the problems of yesterday became assets – the enjoyment of curries, the music of the sitar and more recently the delights of Bollywood/Hollywood. But still the Asians kept their distance which was not surprising if you remember the culture shock they were enduring.

Parents did not allow their daughters to go out on their own shopping or to see their school friends. Whenever socialising there was always the brooding presence of the family around them saying: *They ought to know our own ways and not the gora permissive culture. We like to remain Indians and must teach our children our customs, extended family system.* It was important to mark religious festivals like *Raksha Bandhan* – the Hindu festival that celebrates brotherhood and love. The word Raksha means protection, while Bandhan is the verb to tie. Traditionally, during the festival sisters tie a *rakhi*, a bracelet made of interwoven red and gold threads, around their brothers' wrists to celebrate their relationship.

Socialising was, and remains, a close family affair and on each occasion important lessons are taught and learned about tradition, culture and the correct way to behave. So the leap from rural India to the free-living style of Carnaby Street in London was enormous. And the change was not just about fashions.

In the Asian family tradition sex is not a plaything but has a significant moral and spiritual importance; the ancient India sexologists like VatSayana, Rishi Kokva, Kalyanmal Padamishiri were regarded as saints and philosophers. They studied sex as an essential factor in human life and presented their view in a manner that is not vulgar or shameful. The Sun Temple of Love in Orissa, built by King Nara Simha Dava in AD 1238, the Shiva Linga Temple in Nepal or the frescoes of Ajanta and Ellora caves are all examples of the free and uninhibited nature of ancient Hindus, exhibiting robust beauty, the softly contoured female figures with exuberant vitality and the healthy breath of life. Thousands of sculptures, paintings and poetical compositions like Gita Govinda all have a religious flavour and relevance.

The Indian mind is, therefore, greatly influenced by these ancient traditions and even in modern urban life sex is something which is not normally a subject for family discussion or a topic of social conversation. It is almost taboo between adults of the opposite sex and there is hardly a chance for father and son to discuss such matters.

For many years I wrote a column in two Punjabi publications – the *Punjabi Times* and *Des Pardes*. I was fortunate enough to receive awards and more than 200,000 people in Britain and Europe became avid readers. I say this not to boast but to provide a contrast with how it was when I first started writing about love and sex. To begin with one dared not mention the word 'sex' or even 'family planning'. I even invented a new vocabulary to describe parts of the body so in discussion the 'real' words need not be used. When I wrote about the importance of birth control, the younger women were delighted, but the elders, who decided the fate of the younger members of the family, were furious and they burned all the copies of my publication they could find. I was accused of corrupting the minds of their innocent daughters and daughters-in-law. Years later, the same people honoured me as 'Priestess of Love'.

This was the moral mentality back in the fifties and you would be surprised how the level of ignorance of 'the basics' persists today. What then should the new arrivals do when faced with the open promiscuity of Western culture? Certainly in the fifties and sixties Asians felt greatly embarrassed and perplexed to be part of what they perceived to be a corrupt society. Parents would prevent their children from having anything to do with their English classmates. They looked on their children with suspicion in regard to sexual matters and the consequences for transgressing traditional mores were harsh. The polarisation of schools now makes crossing the racial divide less of a problem but parental control it seems is as tight as ever particularly among girls.

This letter is typical: *I am a Muslim girl, nearly 18 years old. My parents are so strict that the only time I can leave my house is when I go to college. I thought I could handle it, but now I've reached this age I feel I need some freedom and independence.*

Pre-marital sex is certainly forbidden for girls in most of the Asian groups regardless of religion. Even today, families will turn to violence against their own daughters and sisters – it is always assumed the female is at fault – if extra-marital sex is discovered or worse they are found to be pregnant. And a discovery after marriage of early sexual involvement of the bride will result in marriage break-up. Of course freedom when it comes can be surprising for all concerned, not least to the individual seeking more freedom: *I am a young guy who comes from a strict family. Last year I passed all 3 of my A levels. My parents were so happy and proud of me. The problem is that while I was at college I met a guy the same age as me who I developed a very warm and loving relationship with. Now that I am working and doing well for myself my parents want me to settle down with a 'nice girl' whether she be my choice or not. I don't really know how to tell them the truth as I know that they will probably never speak to me again.*

As Asian families, or rather Asian parents, see it, the Western approach to life is too undisciplined; one must get good qualifications which in turn leads to a 'proper' job ideally in one of the professions – law, medicine or accountancy. This may not be unique to Asian culture but it is often accentuated and young people are not encouraged to deviate from the path: *I am an Asian boy in my last year at school and am interested in becoming a photographer, but the thing is my parents have always wanted me to be a doctor or a lawyer, but I am not interested in either of them. I can't handle the pressure or the expectations from my parents. I don't think my parents will listen to what I have to say as they've got so many plans for me.*

Times have moved on though and those quiet, discreet get togethers to remember the old days have been transformed at the top end of the economic spectrum where now five star hotels will be taken over for lavish events marking high days and holidays like Diwali or some awards ceremony of which there are many. The modest local hall of the early days hired to celebrate a wedding with perhaps a hundred guests celebrating on crisps, peanuts, Bacardi, brandy and whisky have been replaced with lavish functions attended by five hundred or more with no expense spared in entertainment and hospitality.

Asians now feel completely confident in their own achievements and rightly so; there is no false modesty at these gatherings, the full regalia are on display. These are moments for Asians to celebrate and white faces are few and far between. Why should they be there, it has nothing to do with them? Well it does and it doesn't. Very often at these events praise is given to the host nation for providing people with the opportunity to succeed and, more often than not, a trophy chief guest – a white politician or even a member of the royal family – is invited along as an adornment. But make no mistake, this is not to say look how integrated we are, rather it is to say look how important a figure we can invite to our event. Ego runs high in the Asian world. To be fair, a little back-slapping is in order as there can be no dispute that the achievements of the Asian business community are considerable, but what it is doing is increasing the divisions between white and Asian and between the haves and have-nots within their own communities.

Scratch the surface among some Asians and you will find old battles are still being fought. They rage against the Raj and yet adopt so much of the British style; they accept all the advantages and opportunities of living and working in Britain and still complain about prejudice against them. They say they are being refused access to top jobs in the civil service, prevented from running for the plum parliamentary seats and if they do get voted in, failing to be promoted to high ranking status within the parties. One has to ask why and the answer seems to be simply because they are not one of us. But how can they be one of us if they never mix apart from on official business? Occasionally in the judiciary or in parts of London someone will rise to the top but they are few and far between.

On the other hand, you have the white British who will moan about how the neighbourhood is declining and yet take for granted such basic facilities as late night shopping which were in large part due to Asians working late every day of the week. This type of dedication convinced the large supermarkets that they had to offer the same service. The old British work ethic has been forced to change precisely because immigrants, and not just Asians but now also East Europeans, are prepared to do the work more efficiently, more cheaply and more promptly. In short life has changed for everyone, it is called evolution. That is the good part.

Where it has plainly gone wrong is that for some reason we are not prepared throw open our doors and welcome our neighbours without condition, without reservation and without pre-judgement. David Goodhart writing in the *Guardian* newspaper said: *Social psychologists also argue that the tendency to perceive in-groups and out-groups, however ephemeral, is innate...They argue that we feel more comfortable with, and are readier to share with and sacrifice for, those with whom we have shared histories and similar values. To put it bluntly – most of us prefer our own kind.*

The native English have entirely accepted Indian food, spices and cooking, they seem to enjoy their music and they like their films which above all seem to have crossed the divide. Plays with an Indian theme play to packed houses in our national theatres so what is holding us back? Why do we enjoy the performance but fail to enjoy each other's company after the show? Is it that most basic point we cannot see ourselves ever becoming intimate with someone from another group and therefore we are just not interested in making the effort?

As in so much the social trend will be set by the young and it is the young who have to break down the barriers before they become too high. There are some small shoots of optimism in the undergrowth.

One correspondent berated her sister for failing to shake off what she saw as 'the old ways': *We were both born and bred in Scotland and I cannot understand why my sister is sticking so strictly to the Asian culture and now even putting her daughter through the same heartache.*

Perhaps one of the greatest obstacles to social integration is because the role of the female in Asian society is secondary to that of the male. The household revolves around the demands and needs of the husband. Although it has undoubtedly made some inroads in the major cities, Women's Lib never made any impression on most of Indian society which still remains predominantly rural. Its influence on Indians living in the UK in the early days was probably also limited because most then kept a low profile. Even women's official status is inferior as so many do not have a permanent UK immigration status which they believe adversely affects their rights – not least in seeking redress from bullying husbands. They do not call up their female chums and say: 'Let's go to a movie. I'll tell my husband he can put something in the microwave tonight.' As husbands control the finances and own the properties there is little scope for female rebellion.

In white English homes it is commonplace for wives to organise parties and more or less tell their husbands that an evening has been arranged. Socialising does not work like that in Asian society because the whole purpose of socialising in this world is to network, advance the business, grandstand in front of colleagues or in some other way advance the male's position or career. One Sikh put it plainly: *We don't socialise – it's all business.* No white woman today would tolerate attending a gathering just to watch their husbands mingle and drink while they sit quietly in the background. The days when the women retired from the dining room to go and powder their noses while the men talked serious 'stuff' over brandy and cigars have long since vanished. Maggie Thatcher was always considered the only 'man' in her cabinet and much changed from the day she walked through the door of 10 Downing Street. But it was a double-edged sword because, while she created further opportunities for the Asian community to flourish in a winner-takes-all climate, the Asian men were not happy about what they saw as the encouragement for women's independence and greater self-confidence. After all if a woman can run the country why should they sit at home and wait for their husbands? Today it is perfectly true that Asian women have built their own businesses but for the vast majority not a great deal has changed in most Asian homes; it is perfectly normal to visit someone's house and realise that the 'women' are there but keeping out of sight in the kitchen.

The typical lot of an Asian woman does not seem appealing

to a white English person – male or female. Economically dependent on their husband or in-laws, she is under constant pressure from her own parents to go through sometimes very difficult times with patience and perseverance in the belief that the problems will soon be over. Asian women are brought up to be obedient daughters-in-law and to make sacrifices for the sake of the family. One woman, desperate and unloved, sought an explanation in her faith: *I try not to look at myself in the mirror. I feel so crushed and crumpled inside, unwanted, undesired – maybe I have sinned in the past life and therefore deserve this suffering.* The mother-in-law syndrome is very powerful in Asian society and some wives suffer in silence and then, when they have married sons of their own, dish out the same medicine to their daughters-in-law.

One of the great opportunities for Indians coming to the UK was the ability to escape the shackles of the *caste* system; in India everyone has their place, traditionally there are only certain jobs people from the 'lower castes' can do. The spin on the system is that it ensures everyone has the exclusive right – the monopoly if you like – on particular work which is fine so long as the monopoly you enjoy does not include clearing the blocked sewers – a task which is performed 'exclusively' by the so-called untouchables. For those at the top of the tree, the *Brahmans*, their superiority is entrenched still further. Socialising between castes and inter-marrying is of course forbidden. In the UK, the white British make no such distinction and if an Indian of any caste is able to do a specific job that is acceptable. However, within their own community the hierarchical structure is preserved. In modern India there is said to be a weakening of the caste system, but old ways die hard in the same way as it will take a long time before the social structure in the UK changes.

It is possible for Indians to escape the suffocating controls of the caste system. In Canada anecdotal reports say it simply does not matter; you are just Indian. One married woman who went to Canada as a refugee along with her family and who now lives in the UK said it was only on her return to the UK that Indians asked about her caste as her married name gave no clue as to her origins. She protested: *What does it matter? I am a human being. It was never an issue when I lived in Canada. There must be something about England which brings out this class and caste issue in people.* In fact she was a Brahman.

In Britain – England in particular – the class structure is as enduring as the caste system in India; an Englishman knows his place, they say. There is upper, middle and lower class and instinctively an Englishman knows where he and more importantly everyone else belongs. Snobbery abounds so if the English find it hard to get on with say a 'nouveau riche' neighbour who has made his money rather than inherited it but still speaks with the wrong accent, what hope is their for a 'foreigner'?

Increased affluence and prosperity have helped many Asians cross the invisible divide; many do a great deal of noble charitable work and some are even elevated to the peerage or knighted in recognition of their efforts. But they are the exceptions to the rule and even they still feel themselves somehow apart from the white English community.

By nature man is tribal; we know our own kind, we know who we can trust and, while we may not actually be at war with the rest, we will always keep them at arm's length. In its most raw form we need look no further than the Middle East where nations rapidly descend into violence, split along tribal lines, when law and order fails. Perhaps the rest of the world should pay closer attention?

In reality though there is something closer to home for us to study – ourselves. We could do a lot worse than consider the little battles which we fight daily against one another, even within our own families – the harsh word and the gossiping; the refusal to welcome a neighbour; the open warfare on the roads when we drive aggressively; the battle to get to the front of a queue knocking others aside. It is always 'me first'. But what difference can an individual act of kindness make on the rest of humanity? The answer is a great deal.

There are places in India and Britain where the caste and class systems have vanished and that is in the most deprived slums and on the streets. When man has been stripped of all his airs and graces, when his most prized possession is perhaps a ragged shirt or a pair of worn out shoes salvaged from some rubbish dump, then any such artificial status of position in society magically evaporates. It becomes a question of survival when all must help each other for the common good. It is the ever popular metaphor of the tamarind tree. Compared with other trees it only has small leaves, so what shelter can each leaf offer from the sun? Individually not much, but the leaves of the tamarind tree are packed closely together and therefore provide all the shelter anyone could need.

Chapter Five

The woman's voice and inter-marriage

Khudi Ko Kar buland itna
Ki har takdir sa pehle
Khuda bande se yeh puchhay

(Make yourself so great
That before determining your destiny
God must ask you: Tell me what is your desire?)

Is this true of Indian woman? Probably not. She is still very much a second class citizen particularly in rural areas in India and it is probably not much better in the UK. She has no voice and there is no-one to ask their opinion or share her desires. It is particularly true in the early years of Indian marriage, even though it might change later in a woman's life.

Women have been seen as incarnations of both the highest good and the basest evil. Seldom have they been perceived simply as human beings. Society has evolved myths to explain and reinforce their powers and weaknesses. In the classical literature woman is valued as a *samsara-hetu* – or 'source of the world'. Biologically people have not changed since the days of hunter gatherer societies, but their social positions have varied tremendously.

Significant differences have existed in expectations regarding women's appropriate patterns of behaviour, privileges and responsibilities and the value attached to the woman's role. Some sociologists present a picture of man's domination over women as stemming from evolutionary adaptations of early human beings to a way of life based on hunting and warfare. In their view, the genetically imprinted male dominance continues to shape relations between the sexes today. Others point to a period when men reacted by subjugating women, a condition that remains with us today.

If anyone questions the lowly status of women in India then the story reported in *India Together* in September 2006 should dispel any doubts. Near a private hospital in Paltran, Patiala district, 50 dead female foetuses were found at the bottom of a 30 foot well. The article said: *The story is every bit as horrific as it sounds. But it seems to have passed off as just another sad incident of the way women remain unwanted and continue to be hated and undervalued in this country.* According to reports quoted in *The Times* in July 2007, it was estimated that ten million female foetuses had been aborted in India in the previous twenty years.

In parts of India, where there are so few young girls, impoverished parents are even selling their daughters as Shreela Flather noted in her book, *Woman – Acceptable Exploitation for Profit* (Whittles Publishing, 2010): *In parts of Haryana, a state in northern India, there are about 770 girls for every 1,000 boys and the consequence of this is an increase in female trafficking; 100,000 women were sold in 2002, according to UN figures. So girls from other states and even from outside the country, known as paros, are much in demand. The poorest families facing starvation are selling their own daughters, reversing the dowry system. They might accept $50 if it means finding food to survive – the price is higher if the girl is younger. Initially they may be sold as brides, but all too often they are then 'traded' like some commodity into sex work or as slaves.*

And yet in ancient Indian culture there was not only equality of the sexes in marriage but in the home the woman's place was the exalted one. Rig Veda (85,26) pronounces: *Go to thy home so that you may best be thy household's mistress; a ruler of the house – then will address the assembly.* Things are not quite like that now, but as we shall see, the woman's voice is growing louder in society and when it comes to marriage they want to be heard.

In the early Vedic society of India, woman occupied a dignified place. Great sanctity was attached to the institution of marriage and a wife was regarded as the mistress of the household. She was styled *Sadharmi* and no religious ceremony could be consummated without her active participation. She was considered as the embodiment of female cosmic energy. The Pardah system, also known as Purdah was started by the Muslims and only later adopted by the Hindus, was conspicuous by its absence. It involves the seclusion of women from public observation by wearing a veil or by the use of high-walled enclosures, screens and curtains within the home. But in earlier times Indian women had considerable freedom in their choice of their marriage partners. They took part freely and openly in feasts and festivities. Women were not debarred from acquiring education and spiritual knowledge. Widow remarriage was prevalent and permissible; today there is scandalous neglect of widows who are prevented from remarrying. This can be doubly traumatic if a child bride is betrothed to a man or even young boy who dies before the wedding day. In these circumstances she is regarded by some as a widow even before formal marriage.

During the medieval period a marked deterioration in commoner women became discernible as they were reduced to pathetic figures steeped in ignorance and superstition; there was child marriage, sati, pardah and female infanticide – we seem to have come full circle on this last point today.

Guru Nanak, the founder of Sikhism and a notable social reformer, campaigned against what he saw as the pernicious evils being perpetrated against womankind. He questioned the very basis of the idea of treating women as inferior. He said:

By woman, man is conceived
Of woman, he is born;
With woman, he is betrothed
and married;

With woman he embraceth friendship;
With woman goeth through the world;
When one woman dies another is sought for;
To woman he is bound;
Why call her bad from whom are kings?
Of woman everyone is born;
None may exist without woman;
Nanak, only the Lord is independent of woman.
(Mohalla 1, Asa Di Var)

Since the mid-80s, there have been more inter-caste and inter-religious marriages. Like all other marriages, these have been the same – some happy, successful, loving and caring while others have failed. No-one really knows whose fault it is when they fail; there are probably as many reasons as there are marriages. But it has to be said that inter-caste marriages are not widely accepted. They are not only frowned upon, but are considered to dishonour the family. Such feelings have not totally disappeared but they are reducing. A mother who was fed up with her own marriage called to say what she had told her grown up daughter: *My own marriage has failed because of my husband's drinking. I advised her to find herself a white man who would love and care for her.*

But marrying a non-Asian for some families is just as big a disgrace as marrying someone from a different caste and the entire family is affected. Parents, uncles and aunts are distressed saying the son or daughter is turning their back on their religion and their culture. The blame is thrown around. In one instance, which was typical, a brother-in-law got furious with his sister-in-law calling her a careless mother who did not have any control over her children. Why did she allow her daughter to bring such humiliation on the family? Why did she let her daughter go out on her own to make friends with goras? But what could the mother have done? Her daughter had done well at school and gone to university, she could not have been chaperoned wherever she went.

In this instance the fight came to a head when the girl's own father threatened to kill both her and her boyfriend should they get married. The girl listened to the storm bursting around her and the next morning went off as usual to university. She never came back. A week later she phoned to say she had got married. Pressures being what they are on young girls it is not surprising to know that girls run away from home every week.

Another sad story was of a mother who called during one Easter Week. *We are parents of three daughters. The oldest was married and then divorced because her husband was violent. After a couple of drinks his mood changed rapidly and he would become abusive and violent. After suffering so many cruelties, our daughter was divorced. The second daughter ran away a few months ago and now our third daughter hasn't come home since leaving for school.* The distraught mother was advised to call the police but she refused in case word got out and further disgrace befell the family.

The following sorry tale seems to encapsulate the whole culture clash. An Indian mechanic got friendly with the daughter of the white English boss in the garage where he was working and they married. He kept it a secret from his own family and it was not long before the girl became pregnant and had a daughter. For a while this clandestine life worked until his own parents, completely oblivious that they were already grand-parents, decided that it was time for their son to get married and settle down. He broke the news to his wife and said they would have to divorce because he dare not tell his parents that he was married to a gori as they would be angry and never accept the situation. His wife pleaded that at first it was the same with her parents but that they had come to accept him because she seemed to be happy. But he rejected her pleas saying he was scared of his father and mother who would be devastated if they knew that he had been seeing her for so long and had fathered a child. He said: *They will not accept you. We are not like Brits. Their parents do not interfere with their children's happiness. They will do anything to see them happy. Indians are heartless. They only think of themselves, their traditions, their culture and their family. They will engage me soon and get me married. I am not prepared to argue with my parents.*

The tirade continued. His parents considered white girls, goris, to be useless. They break up Indian families by taking husbands away to live on their own. They do not respect their in-laws. In short their upbringing and breeding means they cannot fit into Indian society. White women are good for enjoyment but not for wives.

A sad story which ended in divorce, but some inter-marriages have worked well with all the family happy and contented. Usually if a girl marries a white boy there is less of scene, but it is the son who marries outside the Indian community which causes the greatest upset. The reason is in large part because parents expect their sons to care for them in their old age.

According to tradition, Indians live with their sons and not with their daughters. This makes boys more obedient and loyal to their parents who, perhaps from a small income, have educated their son, found him a job and in all probability found him a wife too. He believes he owes everything to his parents and for this reason he likes to stay in his parents' house. He will always listen to his mother in preference to his wife, who of course has no-one in the house to back her up. The 'little boy' can do no wrong and behind the closed doors there is often much violence and abuse as husbands berate their wives over the real or imagined offences against the mother.

The mother son relationship is dealt with sharply in Gurcharan Das's book, *India Unbound*. He cites the psychologist Sudhir Kakar who has analysed Indian childhood. *Kakar said that it begins with the Indian bride who is not fully accepted in her husband's home until she produces a male child. She is so grateful when a son is born that she indulges him to excess. As the boy grows up, he remains close to the mother and distant from the father.*

The end result is that the boy grows up narcissistic and has a weak ego.

A mother symbolises sexuality and creativity, she is also depicted in ancient Indian literature as 'the highest guru'. It says: *If one has a mother, he is sheltered, he grieves not, age does not weigh on him even though fortune may betray him. Even a man at the end of his hundredth year, if he takes refuge with his mother, he acts like a child of two years.* A mother therefore is valued, feared and respected by the son in the effort to repay her with affection and protection. The fact that sons are a source of security in their old age, they carry on the lineage and that mothers make a greater emotional investment in them no doubt explains why daughters are less valued. Scanning of pregnant women has had another dangerous impact on women. Although this is 'women against women' this fact is ignored by the mother and there is greater pressure on the pregnant woman to abort if she is carrying a female child. There is already an imbalance in the number of women and men in many parts of India.

The parents' investment in their sons does not always pay dividends. The tradition of caring for their parents is slipping and organisations like Shelter in the UK report increasing numbers of elderly Asian people being abandoned by their children; the same trend is happening in India where the young, newly affluent offspring do not want their lifestyles cramped by aged parents. There was a terrible story reported of a son who had delivered his frail mother to a crematorium in Delhi, but she was saved only when staff saw her moving.

Although people have become more relaxed about inter-marriage – in fact according to a census by the Policy Studies Institute Britain has one of the fast growing mixed-race populations in the world – there are still objections, some on religious grounds but also over minor issues like food and behaviour in front of parents and in-laws. In Indian society you do not do things in the presence of your parents such as kissing and cuddling or sitting on your boyfriend's knee.

Asian mothers living in Britain prefer to find prospective daughters-in-law from India because they know what is expected of them; to the mother it means another helping hand about the house who does not have to be paid. This is where much of the misery lies and it is little wonder that white girls want to have little to do with it. They are also less likely to put up with waiting hand and foot on their husbands; there are not many Indian men who would return home from work and be happy to prepare their own dinner or help put the children to bed. Young brides who find themselves in an unfamiliar Britain have written about their tragic lives often under the subjugation of their mothers-in-law. The husbands, of course, back their mothers with scarcely any consideration of loyalties to their wife. There are stories of abuse, womanising, gambling and alcoholism which, while not confined to the Asian community, are harder to endure alone.

One young bride wrote to say she was being treated as a virtual slave and the worst offender was the so-called 'aunty'. These aunties – in reality often only friends of the family – are the most treacherous operators. Typically they impress their village friends back in India and persuade them to send their daughters to be married to their son, or perhaps a 'highly suitable' nephew. Invariably these marriages are a disaster as aunty fails to go into detail about the prospective bridegroom's character or educational background. In this instance the new bride said: *My husband refuses to give up his English girlfriend and spends weekends with her. If I ask questions I am beaten. I am not allowed to leave the shop and I have to do everything 'auntie' tells me.*

One of the serious problems facing newly married couples, which is only accentuated if it is a mixed marriage, is background; this might include the social, educational, cultural differences as well as race. Girls arriving from India are often completely out of their depth. Similarly girls educated or born in England suffer from multiple psychological complexes. Language and social patterns of partners from the two countries inevitably vary greatly. Inferiority leads to suspicion, fear, anger, separation and finally divorce. Women face particular hardship when marriages break down. Some parents regard the marrying off of their daughter as a problem off their hands. The last thing they want is for their daughter to come knocking on the door asking to be taken back into the bosom of her own family having been thrown out by her husband or having walked out of her own accord.

There is probably a need in every major UK city for organisations to look after Asian one-parent families, divorcees and other people who suddenly find themselves at the mercy of others. Sadly the so-called elders of the society are perfectly well aware of what is happening to these young people but when it is brought to their attention they blame society for corrupting young Asian girls.

The multicultural and multiracial conflict and confusion in the UK has been responsible for many divorces in the Asian community. The domination of mothers-in-law has been mentioned but Asian men also show weakness and irresponsibility in not standing up for their wives and, indeed, for themselves. This lack of response is driving women away from unloving, uncaring and immature relationships.

The problem is particularly highlighted in Western countries as Asian women are exposed to other marital styles and, by comparison, their relationships seem restricted at best. Asian men have one standard for themselves and another of subjugation for their womenfolk. Jealousy, suspicion, unfaithfulness and violent behaviour continue to destroy marriages. While suspicion is not a new phenomenon Asian men are peculiarly smitten by it and it does not appear to lessen with age. One correspondent wrote: *It was painful in my younger days, but now, when*

I am a grandmother and approaching fifty, my husband's mind is still as prejudiced as ever towards me. I have tried to convince him that all my life I haven't looked at another man because that's not my nature. No matter how unhappy and frustrated I have been the idea of another man or extra-marital relationship has never crossed my mind.

It seems women cannot win. If an Indian man is educated he puts on airs and graces if his bride comes from India and accuses her of being ignorant and only fit to work in the kitchen. If she has been living in England it can be worse. One young wife wrote of her husband's accusations: *He said I was brought up in Britain, a country without any standards or restrictions on girls, like in India. He said you must have been sleeping with your English friends, having fun, you are an experienced girl.*

When eventually she became pregnant he shocked her by saying: *I am going to tell the hospital doctor that this child is not mine.* Or on another occasion: *Have the child and I will take it home to my Mum and Dad in India otherwise she will also become a slut like you.*

It is fair to say that the marital scene in the younger generation is becoming more complicated and, from the perspective of an agony aunt, modern trends are not working. As we become cleverer with our technologies and our know-how, I feel the younger generation are going through increased turmoil in their personal lives and the traditional guidance they might have expected from their family now seems irrelevant to them.

We live in an age of anxious confusion and cultural ferment where morality is no longer an endowment of culture. Sexual impudence and moral decadence are slowly going beyond social admonition. What was once regarded as the sacrosanct institution of marriage is increasingly threatened with so-called free living. The anti-marriage syndrome is gaining currency among many young people. While this is still a predominantly urban phenomenon confined to the major cities, it is a contagion which is bound to spread. Part of the reason is that a growing minority of couples no longer believe in marriage because they feel cohabitation for a few years first is a more appropriate way of deciding if they are compatible. But even then some people are no further forward. One woman wrote of her marriage after a 'trial' period together: *My husband is a closed book to me. He tries to be straightforward but there is always something which prevents him from sharing his ideas with me. We are not strangers to each other, but he remains to be his own person.*

For some Asian women, however, determined to succeed in life, they believe their only option is to marry a non-Asian. The writer, Yasmin Alibhai Brown, herself married to a white man, said recently: *Rightly or wrongly quite a lot of us [British-Asian women] believe that in order to fulfil our lives it just won't be possible if we marry an Asian man who however egalitarian before marriage very often becomes extremely sexist afterwards.*

Women are increasingly aware of their rights and position; they are not as submissive as their mothers who are prepared to tolerate the chauvinistic behaviour of the husbands as well as their fathers and brothers. In the middle and upper classes they mix more with non-Asians, albeit on a superficial level and there is no escaping the mass-media today where nothing is left to the imagination. I would not want to be considered a feminist or anti-male in any way but many problems are caused by men stubbornly refusing to accept that women are changing, have changed; they expect to do more, they are increasingly showing that they can achieve more and men should no longer expect them to remain the quiet, submissive type hiding in a back room while the men get on with the important matters in life. This is somewhat akin to life in Victorian England when women were regarded as a source of cheap labour in the lower classes and, in the middle classes, were restricted to managing the household servants and doing the occasional bit of charitable work.

Inter-marriage is not a peculiarly Anglo-Asian issue, such mixing of the races has long been discouraged in America for example; it was not until 1967 that the laws preventing freed Black slaves from marrying whites – anti-miscegenation legislation as it was called – were repealed by the US Supreme Court as being unconstitutional. At that time 38 states still had active laws prohibiting non-whites from marrying whites. By this time, of course, many US servicemen had returned from fighting in the Vietnam War with Vietnamese girlfriends and brides.

The complexities of an Indian marriage are intriguing and, in themselves, divisive. In the Hindu tradition, for example, there are eight separate categories of marriage. The most highly regarded type is *Brahma* in which a boy's parents ask the parents of a girl from a 'good family' if they will give their daughter in marriage to their son. The aim of the Brahma marriage is the mutual advancement of the two families. They also believe that such a holy marriage saves twenty-one generations of the bridegroom's ancestors from hell. No dowry payment is made.

The least regarded was the rite of *Pisaka* – when a man seduced a girl and effectively kidnapped her. This is of course illegal but it is interesting that it had its own category. The marriage purely for love – the *Gandharva* marriage – comes well down the list and is considered inferior because it is inspired by lust.

Then there is inter-marriage between different racial and religious types. If this is frowned upon so too is marrying above or beneath your social position. Although the demanding of a dowry payment is now illegal in India, one way of keeping social groups apart is the 'price tag' which is attached to certain positions and jobs in society – a Government official is a bigger and costlier catch than say a shop manager.

Contrast such complexities with Britain. Although there are laws, marriage in Britain is considered a personal matter, so are marital relations and family life; whether religious or civil, marriage in practice is viewed as a contract. You can contract in or you can contract out. Widespread use of pre-nuptial agreements are still some way off for Indians.

But it is worth looking a little more closely at the question of dowries which, despite the law, continue to be a source of much misery in families; dowry related deaths, violence and suicides are still regular occurrences and the subject of many letters to an agony aunt. Over 12,000 dowry deaths were recorded across India in 1998/99, the highest number of cases were in the poorer eastern states of Uttar Pradesh and Bihar.

Britain has also spawned it own particular dowry crime wave. Police are investigating claims of thousands of British Asian men marrying Indian women and then abandoning them, after taking dowries from their brides' families. They say they have to return to the UK to organize visas and then the hapless brides never hear from them again.

The offerings of dowries and bride-prices – the payments can go both ways – used to be commonplace the world over, but in India the practice seems to be out of control. An agony aunt is often asked to help find a suitable husband or wife and the acquisitive mothers sadly begin at this early stage by asking, *Can you find out how much the boy earns and what his house is like?* These are the inquiries that happen today in London.

Before exchange controls were relaxed in India some families used their children's weddings as an opportunity to acquire goods which they themselves could not afford. Demands were high and the pressures on the brides' families were severe. In rural India landholdings would be sold as parents pushed themselves deeper into debt and in the urban community the family home would be sold. Even after a wedding the demands will continue on the bride's family and failure to pay up leads to severe hardship for the bride who, alone and defenceless in her husband's family home, can be starved, beaten and virtually imprisoned in the house.

However young wives are now fighting back and have taken

advantage of new laws which allow them to report not only their husbands but also their mother-in-laws who are often the instigators of much of the misery. In India's capital, Delhi, a special wing was established in the Tihar jail specifically for mothers-in-law. It was not long before the unit, designed to handle 50 inmates, was overflowing with 150 women.

If the authorities are tackling the dowry scandal, it has been quickly replaced by the moral pressure being put on middle class parents to provide ever more extravagant wedding ceremonies which can continue for days. Wedding organizers are having a field day satisfying the demands of the middle and upper classes, all determined to out do each other in the grandeur and opulence of the festivities.

The hypocrisy of turning a spiritually based event like a wedding into a vulgar display of wealth has provoked outrage in the Sikh community at least. In July 2007 the Delhi Gurdwara Management Committee, the most senior Sikh body in the city, urged all Sikhs to boycott weddings that were not teetotal, vegetarian or over by noon – considered the most propitious time to be married. Furthermore they called for an end to the ostentation which has seen some celebrations running for days with banquets of tandoori chicken, beer, whisky and dancing late into the night which placed enormous financial burdens on the brides' families despite laws prohibiting demands for dowries.

For a society with such deeply entrenched beliefs, standards, and habits, it is little wonder that integration is at best difficult; Indians do not even seem to like each other, never mind the rest of world. They have their own class structure which divides people not only by creed and by caste, but also by where they come from and finally by the ultimate and probably most important divide – wealth. It seems that everything is forgiven and forgotten if the price is right.

Chapter Six

Arranged marriage – for better or worse

I was sixteen last April and me and my Dad went to Pakistan along with a few aunties. I knew I was going to see this boy. Well, this boy is my Dad's sister's son and my Dad's sister has been after me since I was 12. I knew that because we used to get letters from them asking for my Rishta (engagement). So last year I went to Pakistan but I do not like the boy. My parents gave me no choice, I was trapped. My Dad said he would lose respect even though I told him many times I don't like the boy. My parents were very selfish with me. I found out that many other people asked my Dad for my Rishta but my Dad refused without even asking me and left me with his sister's son.

From an outsider's point of view such apparent callous disregard for the personal happiness of a child is enough to make one ask how anyone can possibly get along with such a culture. Arranged marriages are another stick used to beat the Asian people. The media depict it as the most cruel and dehumanising way to treat a daughter. Such sensational media coverage scares and upsets teenage girls who are caught between the crossfire of traditional ways and western culture.

The reality of what one might call the new era of arranged marriages fulfills the expectations of the young while not binding respective men or women to a particular person. Typically parents 'spot' a suitable candidate and they are discussed within the family. After an initial introduction, the couple are free to meet and get to know each other. Nine times out of ten their verdict is accepted and welcomed by the parents.

One highly educated university graduate wrote about her attitude: *I wasn't that kind of girl who would go after the boys. I am homely and I did not want some Romeo. I wanted someone who would take responsibility for my children. An arranged marriage seemed safer. There is something inside me that is so Asian and I do not want to lose it. With my Indian husband and his lovely family, I have it all.*

Another woman viewed her arranged marriage as *'splendid karma'*. She said: *It was easier to survive the bad times and it is great for our children to have families around us. We get so much out of their love, support and wisdom.*

One interesting phenomenon is to receive requests from native British people to help them have an arranged marriage and to seek advice and guidance in finding 'suitable partners'. In a world where one in three marriages ends in divorce who is to say that careful consideration, even research, of the pros and cons of a particular partner is such a bad idea; it looks beyond passion and considers compatibility, background and character. Parents in any family situation are there to advise and it goes without saying that the best interests of the young person should be paramount not some devious scheme for self-aggrandisement of the family or parents.

Tragically some girls think the only solution is to run away from home, but very often they find that the grass is far from green on the other side as one girl wrote: *I got married to my boyfriend as soon as I left home. It was not heavenly for me because my husband does not trust me. He locks me in the house when he goes to work until the evening when he comes home. I have pleaded with him that I am an Indian girl, a faithful, loving and caring girl, please don't be harsh and cruel to me. Nothing made any difference until we had our first child. He was a bit more relaxed and let me go out with our baby. Mind you it has been worse than an arranged marriage.*

During the Vedic times, between 2,500 and 1,500 BC, women enjoyed complete equality with men. They held a respectable position in the family and society. In the family the woman's role of daughter, wife and mother was also respected. She enjoyed freedom of movement and a bride had the privilege of choosing her husband from among the men who were selected by her parents as worthy of their daughter. At this time it was the practice to combine the bride's personal inclinations and parental advice or consent when it came to securing a suitable husband. Divorce was permitted and widows allowed to remarry.

Over the years marriage has changed little in the Asian world. It still remains the duty of parents to find the right spouse for their daughters as well as their sons. More than 98% of Asian marriages are arranged by parents. Love often follows later built on the passage of time and growing mutual respect. I was one of the lucky ones. It worked for me, although I think my husband was ahead of his time. When my articles about love, sex and family planning first started appearing in newspapers with their special vocabulary and the abusive letters began to arrive, he was the first to back me. He said if I believed what I was writing was right and for the benefit of people, then I should continue.

There is no research to prove one way or another whether the arranged marriage process is better or worse than 'leaving it to nature', but there is endless correspondence supporting both approaches.

'*Not all arranged marriages are bad.*' said one happily married bride. '*Basically you enter into it with a clear head, not thinking of your husband as Mr. Wonderful or living in a cloud. It's clear thinking and you work at it. I was given a choice by my parents and I chose the arranged marriage and it works.*' Another was not so sure particularly as she had been brought up in England. '*Why do parents insist on an arranged marriage when the children are born and bred English? Some children are now more English than Asian.*'

This last point illustrates the difficulty of brides and bridegrooms coming from different backgrounds and cultures. Both may be Indian but if one is from rural India and the other from cosmopolitan London there will be problems. One caller said:

Girls who come from the Asian subcontinent to take part in arranged marriages have tremendous pressure put on them and possibly do not share the same culture as the man they have come to marry. Also Asian families living in the UK are very protective of their children and only want them to marry others of their own culture and way of life.

The reality of life is that the younger Asian generation enjoy the freedoms of the West but when it comes to 'settling down and getting married' they will usually choose to marry one of their own and they are prepared to listen to their parents so long as the parents are prepared to listen to their children. One lady summed it up like this: *Asian children have more freedom these days and parents today play more of an introducing role rather than marriage arranger. In the past arranged marriages have generally been more successful than non-arranged marriages.*

Apparent confirmation of a tried and tested system came from one Muslim who wrote saying: *My mother had an arranged marriage. I have an arranged marriage so too has my sister. There is no question of love at first. We liked each other and got to know each other – so we had a bond which has grown to love.* Some marriages can be founded entirely on 'first sight'. A husband said: *I have been happily married for 12 years and we have three boys. I'd never met my wife before the wedding. Arranged marriages work. I am not against young people choosing their own partners, but they seem confused about relationships and responsibility and need guidance.*

In the Islamic culture and tradition, marriage between first cousins is not uncommon. It may be between two sisters' children or sister and brother's children. Half of British Pakistanis are said to marry their cousins. Such relationships of parents do not necessarily help the newly married cousins to love and adore one another. Marriages such as these often breakdown soon after the honeymoon; parents involve themselves in the disputes and bickering which sadly can lead to irrevocable breaks within the family. The daughter-in-law is sent back to her parents and the whole family is divided, abusing and blaming one another.

The other tragic consequence highlighted in a Channel 4 'Dispatches' documentary by Tazeen Ahmad in August 2010 is that according to numerous scientific studies children of first cousins are more likely to suffer from recessive genetic disorders. In her own family she had three deaf uncles and five aunts died in infancy because, Tazeen is convinced, her grandparents were first cousins who married.

The real tragedy of this is that it is not something new. My husband, Gopal, who had 3 PhDs and lectured at the University of Liverpool, was warning families in the Pakistani, Bangladeshi and Middle Eastern communities back in the 1970s of the dangers of close family marriages. Many children were brought to our home suffering from multiple genetic disabilities, including blindness and deafness, and we implored the community to stop first cousin marriages. It is no surprise with the increasing numbers of immigrants from these parts of the world that the incidence of children with these' disorders is rising.

As soon as the dangers are pointed out there is an immediate defensive reaction saying it is just an attack on Islam, which it is not. The simple course of action is for first cousins to check if they are likely to be carrying the particular gene in question. If they are then surely they should be advised not to marry and even more importantly their respective parents should have the wisdom not to apply moral pressure on the couple to wed.

One mother was determined that her son should marry her sister's daughter. Both sisters were married to two brothers. There was a warm and affectionate relationship hence their children's marriage would, it was assumed, further strengthen the loving bond and continue the family ties. Both cousins had grown up together as all the family was in and out of each other's houses every day.

The marriage went ahead but the 'bridegroom' could not bring himself to see his young cousin as a bed-partner although she was happy to enjoy her married life with her much loved cousin. Despite the cajoling from both sides the young man could not be persuaded that his wife was no longer a playmate 'sister' but his beautiful new bride. In the end she returned to her family and the couple were divorced

Another girl aged 16 years overheard her parents discussing her marriage to her cousin who was 25 years old, a widower with three children. They were planning to take her to Pakistan ostensibly for a holiday but then to marry her off. She was not allowed to continue her schooling after 14 because she had had her first period; the girl said this was the normal practice in her community because parents wanted to safeguard their daughters from the 'promiscuous' British society.

The girl could not express her feelings to her parents as she knew that would have led to a beating or being locked in her room in case she tried to run away. She said she was going to take an overdose and did not write again.

What of the alternative or Christian way? Churches are concerned about the increasing fragility of marriage and many churches offer, even insist, on the couple attending some preliminary discussions with the priest about the sanctity of marriage, responsibilities and challenges in advance of the ceremony. But extremes of overreaction can happen: *I had an arranged marriage as such – it was a Christian arranged marriage. We were forced into it. We didn't have sex but our parents found out that we had touched. We were given two options: never to see each other and be damned by the church, burn in hell etc. or be forced into the marriage. It is not just Asian people who have arranged marriages and this all happened very recently.*

Arranged – or assisted – marriage is not as difficult as it is perceived in Britain. It is the forced marriage, in which a girl is made to marry without any regard to her feelings one way or another, which is to be challenged. In these circumstances girls have been killed, committed suicide or run away. But speaking from personal experience this agony aunt can say it does work. It is possible to fall in love at once – after all there is love at first sight. People ask: how on earth can you fall in love with a stranger? But you do. And it is a lasting love and deep affection. There are many questions; one has to learn, adapt and make compromises. Where there are differences you have to overcome them and not argue.

In a marriage you come to accept the habits and whims of your partner, the idiosyncrasies which make them special; perhaps they irritate at first but then they become an essential part of people's make up – you even miss those little ways when they are gone.

The question of getting on with people outside marriage is not the same issue. This is the debate about the difference between tolerance and acceptance. If we say we can tolerate our neighbour that sounds, and probably is, a little grudging; you will accept their being there but with gritted teeth. That seems to be how the different ethnic communities of Britain have decided they will get along. Let the Asians have their peculiar clothes and strange marital practices, but it is not for us. Just let them get on with it so long as they do not interfere with our lives. Is that integration? Is that what we really mean by a multi-cultural society? It is certainly multi-cultural but it is hardly mixed or integrated. Like oil and water in a glass, even if they are thrown in together they will very soon separate. We have discussed university communities in an earlier chapter and admired how students get on with their lives, thrown together into mixed halls of residence and lecture halls, but watch what happens when they are just sitting around chatting; inevitably Arabs, Asians, English, Koreans will gravitate to their own kind. That is just natural, people feel more comfortable speaking their own language, there is no issue about drinking or not drinking alcohol or smoking and no-one comments on your style of dress.

We can tolerate someone wearing a *niqab* or getting drunk but we do not have to like it. It is wrong to force all women to cover their faces but it is perfectly acceptable if some people want to, so long as it does not affect anyone else. Tolerance and acceptance is not the same as approval. Actually there is a strong element of 'through gritted teeth' in acceptance as well which does not necessarily mean you like what is happening around you but you won't complain. For example, there was a time when cricket matches were watched in reverential silence with polite applause at the appropriate time with the occasional muffled 'Good shot!' Now spectators have learned to 'accept' that there will be chanting and whooping and shouting throughout. There is nothing anyone can do to stop it. There is more crowd involvement in the matches and to a certain extent that has increased the crowd numbers and breathed new life into the game – so it has turned out better in the long run. The 'old-timers' may not like it but they have accepted it. You might say they have learned to put up with the noise. But this is the way cricket matches have always been watched in the Caribbean for example with drums banging and hooters blaring. To that extent cricket has managed to integrate itself; certainly players from all round the world have had long and distinguished careers in the British game regardless of their colour. This is not as far removed from the arranged marriage as one might think.

Changes have happened in sport – in this instance cricket – by force of public demand. The stuffy, one might even say pure, style of English cricket has had to learn, adapt and accommodate the noisy, colourful even rowdy 'foreign' game. All may not have accepted it in the sense that they might not approve of the new style, but they have all learned to tolerate it; there is room for both – the leisurely ball by ball radio commentary still survives into the long, late summer afternoons observing the raucous goings-on out around the ground and even at times out in the field. To that extent they have integrated.

If one casts an eye back through history it is easy to find examples of arranged marriages to suit dynasties and royal connections; bolstering kingdoms, making alliances and pursuing all manner of political agenda far removed from personal love. Gradually the practice has changed. What actually is so different today when parents seek 'appropriate' spouses for their own children, even if it is for the greater good of the whole family? The key surely is for all people to understand why other groups behave as they do as a first step towards accepting it, adapting it or, who knows, maybe even adopting it.

Marriage is regarded as sacred in Hindu, Muslim and Christian teaching. In Indian culture the very gods themselves are married – Shiva-Parvati, Rama-Sita, Lord Krishna-Radha. Marriage is not so much a concession to human weakness rather as a means of spiritual growth. It is prescribed for the sake of the development of personality as well as the continuation of the family ideal.

When marriage is successful it transforms a chance mate into a lifelong companion. Marriage is not the end of the struggle, it is the beginning of a strenuous life where we attempt to realise a larger ideal by subordinating our private interests and inclinations. Love demands sacrifices. By restraint and endurance we can raise mere love to almost the spiritual; the perfect relationship has to be created not stumbled across by chance. In the same way the only option for all the ethnic groupings in Britain is to learn to tolerate each other's peculiarities; we will never all approve of or even simply like all our neighbours but we can start by accepting their right to exist. Love your neighbour as yourself the Bible teaches us which is a fine ideal but for most it will be an achievement simply to muddle along without muttering under our breath as we pass each other by in the street.

When Britain first became 'exposed' to the concept of arranged marriages as they were then happening in this country, there was a tabloid media campaign to 'hunt down' examples and portray them as somehow brutal and uncivilized in a modern society. At the time girls became even more confused and wondered if they were doing the right thing. But requests to find suitable spouses came from all levels of society – solicitors, bankers, lawyers, doctors and dentists as well as from their sons and daughters. This continues to the present time as people beat a path to my door and ask for my help.

Before leaving the subject one should make a clear distinction between arranged, or assisted marriages, and forced marriages as they often get blurred and sensationalized. In the UK since 1999, the Government has been trying to find a way of outlawing the practice of forced marriage. It seems extraordinary that it is not illegal; of course rape and kidnapping are but legislators want to find a way of preventing the offence rather than reacting to it after the event. Writing in *India Link International* magazine, Lord Navnit Dholakia said he hoped a new bill, which made forced marriage a civil rather than criminal matter, would prove to be the breakthrough: *When dealing with a problem where fewer than one in ten cases are reported, meaning that the 300 cases reported to the Home Office and Foreign Office are just the tip of the iceberg, the need for sensitivity and respect is all the more necessary. In the diverse communities where forced marriage takes place, it is often parents or close family members who force a victim into marriage. There is a strong chance that the victims of forced marriage would be unwilling to report their own parents, or other family members, if the punishments included jail and a criminal record,* he said.

Tragically when parents believe the family honour is at stake forced marriages can result in terrible consequences. In June 2007, a Kurdish man living in London was convicted of murdering his 20 year old daughter in a so-called 'honour killing' because she had left her husband and fallen in love with another man. The man ordered the killing with the help of his brother and other men. It was reported that the girl had been forced to marry an Iraqi Kurd when she was 17 but it did not work out and she had returned home, later falling in love with another man. It was said in court that the girl's family had decided to kill her because her relationship was with an Iranian Kurd and not a strict Muslim. The Crown Prosecution estimates that there are about a dozen such murders in Britain every year.

The custom of the arranged marriage on the other hand is here to stay, survive and even grow stronger in whatever country Asians find themselves. They have a new self-confidence in their traditions and values which has grown out of their own self-sufficiency and independence. We return to the title of this book: *We Don't Need You Anymore*. Not only do Asians not need the welfare support but they do not need to abandon their own traditions. Love marriages are wonderful when they succeed, but sadly they do not seem to be any more lasting than arranged marriages. In the end it comes down to two people and what they can make of their own relationship. Either way, it takes work.

The last word should go to one woman who said: *I knew my husband only two hours before we decided to get married. Three days later we were married and have remain happily married for 21 years.*

Chapter Seven

Girls and boys go out to play

Teenage pregnancies, single parent families and divorce are all commonplace. As we have seen, family life and the security and support that it offers, is under threat not only in the Asian community but in all society. Behind the closed doors of even the most genteel families there is often misery and violence. Shocking statistics suggest there are hundreds of thousands of paedophiles and child molesters in the UK alone and the debate goes on – should they be treated or locked up? As people from child protection agencies and, indeed, agony aunts know only too well, so many of the abusers are themselves victims of abuse in their youth. Teenage years are difficult enough for young people without the added turmoil of cultural tensions and differences; for the new generation of Asians – now third and fourth – this is a daily occurrence and the same can be said for all the other minority ethnic groups who find themselves in Britain.

Then, of course, each and every group can be broken down into male and female with the females often coming worse off – but it is not always the case. As youngsters of both sexes move into their teens, and possibly even earlier for some, boyfriends and girlfriends become important. Instinctively they will be attracted by potential partners from their own ethnic group but, when thrown into mixed settings such as universities and colleges, inevitably cross-cultural relationships will develop.

Asian men are highly attracted to white women and there are numerous letters from married Asian women in despair as their husbands openly flaunt their English mistresses; one complained to me that her husband had a child by his lover who then started attending the same school as his legitimate children. The attraction for some men is the apparent 'sophistication' as they see it of Western women; they are regarded as being more modern and gradually the men themselves may even adopt English mannerism, styles and dress.

But men are not always the guilty parties. Many women write asking what they should do as they have fallen in love with a white Englishman and cannot bear to be apart from him.

The important point to remember is the background. In the western world young people are exposed to the media – glossy magazines discussing every possible aspect of relationships and the TV, which for most young people has supplanted the traditional advice they once might have received from parents. As a result children are growing up faster and losing their innocence sooner. This is not the place to debate the rights and wrongs of that state of affairs I would just say that growing up 'too fast' is not the blessing young people often take it too be.

In India, Pakistan, Bangladesh and Sri Lanka probably 80% of the population still live in villages where life is static, certainly unsophisticated in the western sense of the word, and where traditions and values remain as strong as they were a century ago. These are close knit societies where everyone knows everyone else. There is no privacy and no one dare break the rules or go against the wishes of the family. 'Sex education' is a guessing game and often a source of amusement where parents and their children share single rooms. Boys grow into manhood, become aroused, but remain childlike in their mentality in sexual matters – in short they do not know how to cope.

One desperate wife wrote of her experience on her wedding night: *I was shocked to know that this man had no idea of the difference between a man and a woman and did not know how to enter into sexual relations. Many months passed that way. Was I supposed to teach him all this? Without the knowledge of his parents I made him see some blue films and gave him a few novels to read...It did not take much time before I realised that his father had kept him under his domination since childhood.*

But today instead of working things out slowly in their villages, many are now suddenly finding themselves travelling overseas to the cities of Europe and America where the sex industry is big business, offering every conceivable temptation and danger.

When parents write to their sons reminding them to return home for their arranged marriage the young men are in a dilemma. Most of them return willingly because they hold their parents in high esteem, but they are unable to speak about their sexual experiences abroad; they may have contracted a disease or they may have discovered that they are gay. Nevertheless, the marriage takes place and only then does the new couple have to face the consequences.

For young men freed from the shackles, as they see the traditional customs and habits of home, they launch themselves in western society eager to spread their 'wild oats'. Letters from teenagers of both sexes complain either that their boyfriends are putting them under pressure to have sex or that their girlfriends are not prepared to go to bed with them. This is not a unique state of affairs for Asian people, of course, but invariably it is the girls who are thinking more about their future lives and future husbands, and they are not necessarily their current boyfriends. This is exactly what Asian parents constantly worry about when they see their daughters growing up and this is why they try to shelter them from the white British community. It does not do much for integration but one can have some sympathy. As I will suggest later integration does not necessarily mean inter-marriage between the races, nevertheless communication and socialising is essential if different racial groups are ever to get to know each other.

In December 2000 a thought provoking report was produced by Professor Richard Berthoud of the Institute for Social and

Economic Research at the University of Essex. His findings showed that Pakistani and Bangladeshi communities were more likely to uphold traditional values of marriage and the nuclear family than any other in Britain, whereas whites and Caribbeans were more likely to be single parents, divorcees or co-habiting.

Professor Berthoud was quoted as saying: *Around three-quarters of Pakistani and Bangladeshi women are in partnerships by the age of 25, compared with just over half of white women. Virtually all South Asians with a partner are in a formal marriage and the proportion of women who have separated or divorced is less than half that recorded among whites.*

His report, *Family Formation in Multicultural Britain: Three Patterns of Diversity*, highlighted striking differences within minority groups and noted that 60 per cent of Asian adults were married compared with 39 per cent in the Caribbean community.

While divorce is commonplace in the West and divorcees are just another grouping in society, it is a cause of great misery and even disgrace in the Asian world. In the interest of the reputation of the wider family, let alone their own, wives will tend to put up with marital difficulties for as long as possible before finally leaving and hoping to return home to their parents. But the stigma of divorce is a heavy burden to bear. Friends and even family members will look down on you and even ignore you as though you no longer existed.

Single parenthood is tough in any society but because of the tendency to have big families, single Asian women of a young age may find themselves alone with two or three children and still be younger than 30. They face another hurdle – welfare support; because of the close-knit community, some may not want to ask for benefits because that in turn brings further disgrace and loss of face, suggesting the family cannot afford to look after its own members.

The Asian Women's Lone Parents Association was launched

in London as *'a symbol to the outside world that this problem is not a one-off, it is not isolated cases, it is not a small insignificant number. The social shifts increasingly impacting on our community mean that this is a growing problem.'*

The size of families is often a source of much criticism of ethnic minority groups who all tend to be lumped together, but the breakdown of each sector is informative. According to the National Statistics Office, Bangladeshi and Pakistani families were larger than families of any other ethnic group; in Great Britain over 40 per cent of these families had three or more dependent children in 2001. This compared with 28 per cent for black African families, 20 per cent for Indian families, and 17 per cent for white families.

Across all groups the number of lone parent families must surely be considered alarming: the proportion of children living in lone-parent families in Great Britain more than tripled between 1972 and spring 2004, to 24 per cent.

According to statistics for 2001, 15 per cent of Indian families with dependent children were headed by lone parents compared with over 45 per cent of black Caribbean, black African and mixed families and 25 per cent of white families. As always the problems in the inner cities are exacerbated and it is estimated that 40 per cent of all families with children living in central London are lone parent families, almost double the UK average.

It may seem hard for young readers today to know that words like 'love' and 'sexy' were unspoken and unheard of less than 50 years ago in most Asian homes. 'Sexy' would have been almost unintelligible; education on such matters was unheard of in the average household. When I started writing my columns on family planning there was outrage that such explicit language could be printed in family newspapers and magazines. Love was considered to be inborn – you did not 'fall in love.' It was cultivated, if you like, and it grew within the companionship between husband and wife.

The great Indian philosopher and second President of India, Dr Sarvepalli Radhakrishnan, said about love and marriage: *We do not love the woman we love, we love the woman we marry.* The paradise garden of love and bliss grows in the human heart. Its roots are in the collective unconscious, its branches in the fairy tales and the great sacred texts with everything provided and nothing demanded in return. Thus, according to the scriptures, *'Woman as a Shakti (spiritual power) is the embodiment of cosmic energy.'*

The problem sadly, as seen from an agony aunt's point of view, is that rather than loving our partners we, and there is no ethnic divide here, tend to love ourselves more than anyone or anything else. As the letters come in the central theme is one of egotism – why can my wife not be more responsive, why can my husband not be more attentive, why can my daughter-in-law not be more obedient, subservient or polite? Intriguingly there is a common solution to so many of these sad stories and it is a solution which we have touched on elsewhere; if only husbands and wives talked to each other more openly (a difficult concept in an Asian family), if only they would listen to each other more attentively, then there would be less friction. When foreigners do get invited to Asian homes they are often surprised by the somewhat gruff tone used by husbands towards their wives – 'Give me a tea' or 'Take that away.' No please and no thank you. It does not have to be like that but women, no matter how sophisticated and westernised they have become still seem to accept it.

Equally if neighbours managed to spend a little more time getting to know one another and helping one another then the suspicions, misconceptions and hostility would also begin to evaporate. In the Christian gospel according to St Matthew the faithful are warned not to judge others lest they be judged themselves and he writes: *Thou hypocrite, first cast out the beam out of thine own eye; and then shalt thou see clearly to cast out the mote out of thy brother's eye.*

Can man and woman be happy or will there always be friction? For the answer to that this tongue in cheek story seems to sum up the facts of life:

God created Adam and Eve and told them to go and enjoy their life together. They went away happily singing. Adam was particularly happy having found an interesting, playful being in Eve. A few days later, they both came back to God. Adam did not seem quite so happy and God asked him what the problem was.

God please take this person, Eve, from me. She has snatched away all my sleep, peace of mind and comfort. I cannot cope with her, please take her back and I will be alright on my own.'

God said 'OK, leave her here'

Adam went away and had a peaceful night. Woke up and found he missed Eve. A day passed but he was miserable. He had a difficult night and in the morning went straight back to God. He said: 'I am sorry, God, please return Eve to me, I could not sleep, I haven't eaten, I am very unhappy. Please give her back to me.'

And on it goes... .

The joy of yoga, which I taught for many years, is that it gives you flexibility, it helps your breathing and your posture and if you persevere it can bring you a sense of peace. Achieving peace and harmony in a relationship is a goal every couple must wish for. The truly spiritual can reach a deeper peace in their meditation which is known as *shanti* in Sanskrit. Few of us can achieve such levels but just as the yogi and the married couple work hard to reach these heights, all communities can make their contribution by working on what holds us together as a nation. Like Adam in the story who cannot manage without Eve and fights when he is with her, so too all our different racial and spiritual groups in fact need one another despite our squabbling. Life will go on one way or another, it is up to us to choose the path of friction or the path or peace.

Chapter Eight

Ghetto mentality

When you are in a strange land, you look forward to being in the company of your own kind, to having a conversation in your native language, laughing and exchanging news or comparing notes about the new country. You welcome the moment of solidarity, getting together in the pub for a drink and a packet of crisps. The natural instinct is to be nearer your own kind of people.

There were many problems which immigrants shared and tried to resolve. Girls in particular were under stress because their parents had strict rules of behaviour for them, although less strict ones for the boys. As we have seen it became too much for some girls who ran away, occasionally they were found and returned home but nothing was said publicly, to avoid any embarrassment. Nevertheless the girls were scared.

Ghetto mentality was a natural phenomenon for the earliest arrivals who came in search of a better life; they were not so concerned about better living standards, they just wanted to earn more than they could at home, which they did. The only leisure time they had was meeting their mates in the nearest pub comparing their wages which were beyond their wildest dreams.

In some situations, after the pub there was also a long suffering wife waiting at home with dinner prepared. Sometimes the husbands would return with three or four friends to share the evening meal. Wives would either keep silent or rows would start often turning to violence.

But most men came to Britain on their own, leaving their wives and children behind, if they had them. They worked long hours and through the weekends to make enough money to pay for their families to join them. But it took several years and, in the meantime, some men had English girlfriends; everyone knew but nothing was said.

When the family arrived they lived in a rented bed-sit with shared bathroom and kitchen. There was no peace. The landladies were critical about the cooking, about the music, about the amount of electricity being used, about wasting water with too many baths.

In time enough money was saved, or borrowed from friends rather than banks or building societies, to buy a house which was very quickly filled with many fee paying tenants. This sort of mutual support was and remains typical of the approach and is wholly natural. Family and friendship is the basic need of society. It preserves traditional values which are essential for society's survival. People's desire for liberation and involvement in worldly activities led to the ancient philosophers of India to propound the body of learning under the names of *Dharma, Artha, Karma* and *Moksha.*

Dharma denotes the appropriate action in a given situation or duty which varies with time, place, sex, age, etc. Artha refers to the acquisitive instinct in man and that which makes him relish worldly enjoyments. Karma indicates sexual and aesthetic appetites, while Moksha signifies self-realisation or spirituality in human beings at the end of life. The aim is to achieve a balance between the material and the spiritual life.

Ghetto mentality is not peculiar to the Asian community in the UK, it is apparent the world over regardless of race, colour or creed. Even among one race division and separation is normal. It is also not new in Britain.

Writing about life in the highly structured Victorian times, Sir Roy Strong in his book *The Story of Britain* said: *Every Victorian city and town had its slum areas where these people eked out an existence. No respectable person would ever enter such a ghetto with-*

out a police escort. Victorian society was rough at the edges but people did not actually go in fear of their lives. Whereas in the previous century and up until 1830 it had been the task of the army, as a last resort, to disperse by force of arms any unruly masses on strike or demonstrating, now it was the task of the police, bearing only truncheons. The fact that towns were divided up into living areas in this way greatly facilitated this task. Any incursion of the poor into the better-class neighbourhoods was firmly discouraged. The rich lived secure within gated and railinged streets and squares. The middle classes were a journey out to the suburbs. The turbulent and deprived elements of society were thus firmly ghettoised.

It is about natural instinct; notice how the colonial British would congregate in compounds and how they and the Americans still tend to build themselves these isolated communities wherever they live. They do it for protection or, one might say, self-preservation. The most recent and violent example of this was the Green Zone in Baghdad where coalition forces gathered behind heavily fortified defences.

But in civilian life, eventually, if the community is thriving and growing, it has to break out of the confines of these groupings. In the late sixties in Britain the more prosperous vanguard in the Asian communities did just that and bought homes in more affluent areas. There was outcry from existing white British residents but if they could settle, others soon followed and soon a luxurious ghetto of extremely wealthy families would arise. The same story was repeated all over the country in Birmingham. Nottingham, Leicester, Manchester, Liverpool and Glasgow

It is important to realise that even within these communities there is a difference between people who arrived in the first wave, as it were, and those who were born and bred in Britain; many of the latter group regard themselves as English, have no knowledge, memory or experience of life in India and do not see how those 'old days' have any bearing on their existence.

So there is this underlying tension, as I have remarked. But others will always regard themselves as immigrants and develop the immigrant complex – never feeling fully accepted by the indigenous community, always being outsiders and many not even speaking the language despite now having spent most of their adult lives in Britain. These people were made to feel as though they should be grateful for what Britain had done for them, appreciate whatever is made available to them and not complain. One young man said: *My father had suffered a lot of humiliation and worked very hard. Once he was not well and asked his foreman for one day's sick leave and he was told to collect his cards and not come back. I was furious. How on earth can one be so cruel and unreasonable to ask a sick man to go on working on the shopfloor?*

Fast forward the conversation to the 21st century and what do we find, remarkable prosperity with Asians topping the lists of the richest and among the most successful businessmen in the country. A small number do manage to break the mould and move into neighbourhoods where they may even be the only Asians but a remarkable number of them simply stay in the same area where they have become comfortable, but it gradually becomes, at least in part, gentrified. It is not long before the electric gates go up to protect the smart cars and grand homes. Sadly they seem to have swapped one form of enclosed community for another slightly more exclusive and private environment.

For the very well off this does not really matter anyhow; they have their friends who, for the most part, are their business associates and they have their work. Nothing else matters. A few might join the local golf club but in all probability almost everyone feels uncomfortable about that – both the individual new Asian members and the rest of the club. Money, of course, will buy you a place on the top table, particularly if the club needs a new building or extension in which case a handsome endowment will always be welcome. This is not just being cynical, everyone recognises the 'game' being played and extracts the maximum benefit from it; the club gets its extension and the new Asian member enjoys the prestige. He can invite his business contacts to the grand surroundings and he has made his point. He has added a smart English club to his CV in the same way as he might try and invite a well-connected director on to his board.

No matter how mink-lined you make it, life cannot exist satisfactorily ignoring the rest of the world. Isolationism is never a solution and community leaders are rightly worried that what amounts to self-segregation will only divide cities and create hostility. Some civic leaders – in Bradford for example which has a history of ethnic unrest– have tried to encourage their citizens to take a pride in their city first and their ethnicity second, a process which even its promoters considered would be *'lengthy, difficult and potentially painful.'*

The danger when we read the ubiquitous Rich Lists is that we assume everyone in the Asian community is doing well; many of them are but within that grouping we call Asian there are differences and, as we noticed in the chapter on education, not all Asians are over-achievers nor entrepreneurial geniuses. But what a deprived community can offer – solidarity, unity of faith, security from racial abuse – is enough to unite people and make them reluctant to leave. Even a poor community will have a temple or Gurdwara and that is sometimes the most important unifying force in a neighbourhood. As more and more Asians move into an area, then the faster white British move out, so the complaint that 'whole neighbourhoods are being taken over' is more a case of 'the neighbourhood has been abandoned by the whites.' There is no easy solution to buck this trend and it is probably a mistake to try and do so. People have got to want to stay.

For those who cannot speak English well, there is a Catch 22 situation; they have little opportunity to practice their English because all their neighbours and the shopkeepers are probably of Asian origin too.

In the last days of Tony Blair's premiership there were calls for a 'National Britain Day' in an attempt to reinforce citizenship and overcome the problem of increasingly divided communities. The then Communities Secretary, Ruth Kelly, and the former Immigration Minister, Liam Byrne, said financial incentives may also be necessary to step up what they call Britain's 'citizenship revolution'. This is simply recognition of what has been apparent for years: different communities in Britain value their own ways, religions and traditions more than the values and traditions of their host nation.

In April 2007 Liam Byrne announced details about the UK's tough new points-based system for immigration. The aim he said was to attract the most talented workers while weeding out those more intent on abusing the system. He said:

> *Migration has to support Britain's national interests. A new Australian style points-based system will be simpler, clearer and easier to enforce. Crucially it will give us the best way of letting in only those people who have something to offer Britain.*
>
> *With the exception of an elite group of highly skilled migrants all other foreign workers or students will need a UK sponsor to vouch for them and help us make sure they are playing by the rules. A new £20 million network of Border and Immigration Agency officers will be making the checks.*

At the same time the Government announced a new Migration Impacts Forum specifically charged with establishing how best to ensure public services can respond and community cohesion can be retained.

Writing in a Fabian Society pamphlet, Kelly and Byrne had both already warned that there was a 'critical risk' that after 40 years of increasing diversity in Britain, communities would start looking inward and questioning their identity. *So instead of em-*

phasising what they have in common with others, they stress the divisions and differences," they said.

> *Our task in Britain, in the coming decade, is not to plan a separation.*
>
> *Nor can it be about assimilation into a mono-culture. Instead we must develop a meaningful sense of what we all – whatever faith, ethnicity and wherever in Britain we are from – hold in common.*
>
> *We need a stronger sense of why we live in a common place and have a shared future.*
>
> *Today, more than at any time since the Second World War, we need a more vigorous debate about what it is that holds us together and how we express these links more clearly.*

How did we find ourselves with such a fragmented society, divided not only along crude white v. black or coloured lines, but also along religious and even divided within communities of the same colour?

Look back to the 1960s and to the Northern mill towns of Britain which were then booming with orders; new technology meant 24 hour operations and only the Asians – Pakistanis and Bangladeshis in this case – would do the work. All the time the inner-city neighbourhoods were changing as more and more Asians moved in and the whites moved out to the suburbs. Then technology improved still further and even the Asians were not cheap enough to cope with the reduced level of technical skills required, so the work transferred to Bangladesh itself. All of a sudden the Asians themselves were out of work and found it difficult to switch to public service jobs. There were accusations of favouritism towards the white job applicants.

Those whites who could not afford to move away took advantage of housing policies which Asians felt were stacked against them. The local authority in Oldham, for example, was found guilty of operating a segregationist policy after an inquiry by the Commission for Racial Equality in the 1990s.

As we have seen, when housing becomes segregated so too do schools and before long whole sections of the community began to feel like second class citizens. The younger generations who regarded themselves as British, having been born and bred in the country, very soon became disenchanted and accused even their own leaders of failing to represent them properly and being too concerned with the prestige of their position as 'leaders of the community'.

The result in the spring and summer of 2001 were violent clashes in Oldham, Burnley and Bradford culminating in a full-scale riot in Bradford with clashes continuing from 7th – 9th July in which 200 police officers were injured. In some sections of the press the Asian community was portrayed as being out of control and the only beneficiaries were the British National Party who more or less said we told you so.

And who was to blame for all this unrest? Everyone and anyone it seems. The rioters were the first in line with everyone joining in the condemnation. Community leaders, probably with more than half an eye on their status in the establishment beyond their own community, blamed a lack of discipline among the youth and part and parcel of that was the decline in Muslim standards of behaviour which was directly attributable to the influence of western values. The Hindus emphasised that this was a Muslim affair and tried to draw a clear distinction between the two Asian groups. So fracture lines appeared as the shifting tectonic plates of ethnic groups crashed into each other. For now they have closed like the fissures of some earthquake which has temporarily subsided. My contention is that the fault lines are still there waiting to rupture again. It is of paramount importance that communities do not become so alienated that they feel they are 'at war' with the outside world, a world which may only be divided by a major road. Such invisible borders already exist, the trick is to maintain diplomatic relations until such time as we can truly accept one another as citizens of the same country.

Am I exaggerating? I don't think so. Do I despair? Never, it has been my lifetime's work to find solutions. In the end we are all just people. They are at the very heart of this, individuals suffering their own private battles which in large part are caused by these cultural differences. One man wrote: *I am suffering from depression and panic attacks. My daughter has run away from home and my son has married a gori. He never comes home. My wife suffers from arthritis and cannot cope with the housework. Our son and his wife live nearby, but are not bothered about our physical disabilities or financial problems.*

In short the Asian system of the extended family providing mutual and long term support is under threat challenged by conflicting values of western society, but at the same time western society cannot but be affected in turn by the increasing diversity of the visitors to our shores. Do we put up our own barriers, hide ourselves away behind our own 'purdah veil' keeping out anything we dislike, do not understand or fear? What will happen on National Britain Day or whatever it will be called? Will it really show a coming together of people of Asian, African, Chinese and English in a great celebration of flag waving and integrated partying? One has to say that it is unlikely. If it is treated as a day off, any celebrations are likely to be as divided along ethnic lines as ever before. Indians celebrate Independence Day of India every year in Britain just as much as it is remembered back in India. Hundreds of people gather in restaurants and hotels to enjoy stirring speeches – not all of them complementary to Britain, but they hold them just the same. No Brit is likely to take offence because white English faces are rarely seen at these gatherings; in the same way when and if we come to celebrate National Britain Day there is unlikely to be much mingling of the races. How can it happen? Would the Bangladeshis and native white English of Bradford get together for a knees-up? The invisible barriers, the screens are already too impenetrable. No-one will make the first move to welcome wholeheartedly an Asian face or a white face into the community. In the poorer neighbourhoods there is too much animosity, even hatred; in the middle class communities there is too much snobbishness and in the super-rich community, the issue is irrelevant – they do not need anyone else.

Chapter Nine
Racism – let's not pretend

Make no mistake, despite the best efforts of Governments to wipe out racism and racial discrimination, it still exists in Britain. It still exists in India and, scratch the surface of most communities, and you will find a degree of suspicion of 'foreigners'. Psychologists would say it is innate. By our very nature as humans we are cautious, even fearful, about others who are not in our 'tribe' if you like. People living in protected areas are safe, but the very fact that they live with some form of security, whether it is just a doorman or a gated compound, reflects the human need to seek protection from others; we are back to the veil, keeping ourselves apart.

But for the average Asian, Britain is a country where he has to be careful, so for that matter does a white English person. Southall for example is a safe place for Asians not so for white people; it is a 'ghetto' where Asians thrive and are powerful. No-one would think of attacking Asians here or even passing a mildly derogatory word against them.

It is not so different in India where some might argue the discrimination is more insidious with the caste system. Let's consider the India class and caste structure.

Hindu society does not exist as such. It is a collection of castes and was a word given to them by the Mohammedans simply to distinguish them. The word Hindu does not exist in any Sanskrit writing before the Mohammedan invasion of India in the 10th century.

The caste system can be traced right back to the so-called Rig Vedic Period (1700–1000 BC) with the Aryans invasion of

Northern India. They originally had two classes, the nobles and the rest – or commoners. A third group *Dasas,* meaning 'darks' was added presumably to accommodate the darker-skinned peoples they conquered. Finally by the end of this period the social structure had become four classes or castes known as the *chaturvarnas,* or 'four colours' with the Brahmins, or priests, at the top and the Shudra, or untouchables, at the bottom.

Collectively castes do not work together under any sort of unified entity and only stand together when threatened from the outside such as in a Hindu-Muslim riot. Each caste eats alone, marries among its own and dresses distinctively. These divisions vary in intensity from place to place and from one society to another; in South India they are very conscious of it. The categories are described in this way in the Vedas – *Brahma created Brahmins from his head, Kshatriyas from his arms, from his thighs he created Vaishya and Shudras were created from his feet.* But to this day there is no possibility of 'rising' from one caste to another.

Bhimrao Ramji Ambedkar, the scholar and jurist, who despite being born a Shudra or Untouchable, rose to great prominence and was the chief architect of the Indian Constitution. He explained the structure of Indian society like this:

1. According to the Brahmins, the Vedas have defined what is an ideal society and the Vedas being infallible, that is the only ideal society which man can accept.

2. The ideal society prescribed by the Vedas is known by the name Chaturvarna.

3. Such a society, according to the Vedas, must satisfy three conditions.

4. It must be composed of four classes, Brahmins, Kshatriyas, Vaishyas and Shudras.

5. The interrelations of these classes must be regulated by the principle of graded inequality. In other words, all these classes are not to be on equal level but to be one above the

other, in point of status, rights and privileges.

6. The Brahmins were placed at the top; the Kshatriyas were placed below the Brahmins but above the Vaishyas; the Vaishyas were placed below the Kshatriyas but above the Shudras and the Shudras were placed the lowest of all

7. The third feature of Chaturvarna was that each class must engage itself in an occupation assigned to it. The Brahmins' occupation was to learn, teach and officiate at religious ceremonies. The Kshatriyas' occupation was to bear arms and to fight. The occupation of the Vaishyas was trade and business. The Shudras' occupation was to do menial service for all the three superior classes.

8. No class is to transgress and trench upon the occupation of the other classes.

Ambedkar was an outspoken critic of Hinduism and converted to Buddhism. From a young age he campaigned against what he saw as the iniquities of the caste structure. For example, Frances Pritchett of Columbia University records that Ambedkar and other Untouchable children were segregated at school and given no attention or assistance from the teachers. They could not sit in the same classroom as other children and if they wanted a drink of water somebody from a higher caste would have to pour that water from a height as they were not allowed to touch either the water or the vessel that contained it. This was usually done by the school orderly, and if he could not be found Ambedkar went without water

Another word for Untouchable or Shudras is *Dalit* which means 'the oppressed' and is used by Dalits themselves to register their protest against the discrimination they suffer.

Not knowing a Dalit from a Brahmin, Britain has been a lifeline to the Untouchables who, with the right opportunity, have made a success of their lives in the country because they are not treated as inferior. If they want to enjoy their children's weddings with great pomp and show, there is no law to stop them;

they can ride on horse back in the traditional Brahmin way to their bride's home – in India such flouting of tradition, if not the law, would require police protection in some places. Nevertheless while the English regard them as just another Indian, members of different castes will still keep themselves to themselves in the UK.

The reality, of course, is that as humans we instinctively seek protection from within our own kind and anything else we learn from our peers and the environment in which we grow up. Safety in numbers.

Are we actually so different; are some races naturally brighter than others? Psychologists point to the fact that IQ tests have been generally improving over recent decades by approximately three points per decade. This is known as the *Flynn effect* after James R Flynn, who noted the changes which could not all be simply explained genetically.

In their book *Psychology* Henry Gleitman, Alan J Fridlund and Daniel Reisberg say: *Some have proposed that this worldwide improvement reflects the increasing complexity and sophistication of our shared culture: each of us is exposed to more information and a wider set of perspectives than were our grandparents, and this may lead to an improvement in intelligence-test scores. A different possibility is that the Flynn effect is attributable to widespread improvements in nutrition. Whatever the explanation, though, this effect is a compelling reminder that intelligence can be measurably improved by suitable environmental conditions.*

The implication is that if you give everyone the same chance in life, plant the same seeds in the same rich soil then everyone will develop and prosper at the same rate. Sadly that is not the case because at its most basic we have different coloured skin, we even smell differently – the Japanese think Caucasians actually smell offensively. So in India the Dalits continue to suffer despite laws prohibiting discrimination. Why? because you cannot simply change people's attitudes by changing the law. It is against the law to demand dowries but the social pressures continue.

A fine example of the contrariness of man was demonstrated in Britain when a law was passed banning hunting with dogs in certain ways. The immediate effect was an increase in those participating in the hunts, with some saying they had never even considered hunting until the Government forced through a law which they considered curtailed their freedom of action. In other words, I may not like hunting but I will defend to the death our right to do so.

Emotions are running high in Britain within the Asian community particularly among the second and third generations. Unlike their parents who, under the mistaken sense of gratitude and insecurity, did not press their demands for justice and fair play, and relied instead on white people to fight for them or wallowed in their own self pity, the new generations, born and bred in Britain, are standing up for themselves.

Sometimes, as we have seen, standing up for themselves in northern towns in the 1990s meant fighting back, unwilling to accept their parents' attitude that they should be grateful to the English for what they had offered the community. Don't rock the boat, in other words. Instead they would meet the violence of white racist thugs with violence of their own. As the gang and thug culture grew so too did other criminal activity such as the heroin culture.

Although the incidence of blatant discrimination and crude racial insults have somewhat diminished over the years, the level of expectation and the sensitivity to discrimination have increased and, therefore, although the second generation immigrant is, objectively speaking, better off than his parents, he still feels discriminated against far more acutely than they did.

The clash between the immigrant and the British culture has predictably resulted in various conflicts both at a personal and impersonal level. These conflicts have been mistakenly classified under the catch-all diagnostic label of 'cultural conflict'. Every time a child displays insecurity or behavioural maladjustment, or appears aggressive, he is diagnosed by social workers, head teachers, judges and others as a victim of cultural conflict. And the experts then fall over one another to find a nonexistent solution for it.

What is called cultural conflict includes a variety of situations, some of which cannot be subsumed under the capacious umbrella of cultural conflict. Often it is a generational conflict endemic in all societies. Sometimes it is a rejection of specific cultural customs, for example arranged marriages. It may be a clash between culture and colour, as when a black child has fully adopted the British way of life, but because of his colour is not accepted as British by the white community. And then there are acute cases where there is a sense of self-rejection generated by white society's denigration of the immigrant's culture; often the dominant white culture encourages an immigrant child, by subtle and not so subtle means, to despise his own culture. He then develops the attitude of self-rejection, self-contempt and with it contempt for his parents. There are countless cases where a child of four or five calls his parents: 'You damn Pakis', or when they are going out to a friend's house, a child will ask their mother 'Are they Paki like you or English like me?'

Is it racist to prefer the company of your own kind? No, if you do not actively do it in such as way that it might offend another person, but could we in Britain ever achieve the same sense of unity as the Americans at least display when they mark their Independence Day on the Fourth of July? If not why not? One explanation offered is that they have less history to 'give up'. They are all settlers apart from the native Indians. England, Britain, the United Kingdom has stood firm and unconquered since 1066. The interesting *vox pops* running on the news channels after the announcement of a possible Britain Day was what you might have expected – a Scotsman saying he felt more patriotic towards Scotland and a pensioner who remembered Empire Day without much fondness. The Brits are a curmudgeonly lot and are not given to much outward show of emotion, hand on heart as the National Anthem rings out; most of us do not know the second verse of the National Anthem but somehow know what being British means. It cannot be earned by some sort of points system as has been suggested – somehow being more British because you speak better English than the next man.

There will always be the racial chants by mindless thugs at football matches or drunks stumbling out of pubs and at the other end of the scale the English will always be cool and re-served towards a new neighbour regardless of the colour of their skin. But the truth of the matter is that most of us would prefer to marry people of the same race, spend our time with people of the same race and work with people of the same race. We are all doing it and will continue to conduct ourselves in that way un-til we learn to consider our neighbours first. Forcing us to wave Union Flags on a given bank holiday and listening to the Prime Minister of the day address the nation in presidential style prob-ably falls somewhat short of that ideal.

Chapter Ten

The faith zone

Do we dare talk about religion these days? Can anyone express an opinion one way or another without being accused of causing offence? It seems not. Britain, once famous for its freedom of speech, is beginning to stutter and stammer when it comes to expressing openly an opinion on any subject let alone religion for fear of not being politically correct.

The agony aunt's post bag is full of life's horrors but where are the religions, where are the references in any of the letters to the support people have received from their churches or temples? If there is a reference it is usually of resignation to their lot: 'it must be my karma.' Correspondence focuses on 'self' and religion, faith or any other sort of belief do not get a look in, but if religion cannot connect with people when they are at their most vulnerable, when can it? Perhaps they have tried it and found it to be wanting and that is when they turn to an agony aunt. An agony aunt is both neutral and yet somehow comforting in the sense that a dear aunt might be comforting; she will try and see both sides of the story and give sound advice. This is the role of mentor – giving direction and correction impartially.

All religions speak of 'peace among men', 'loving one's neighbour' and other acts of kindness but where are the Good Samaritans when there is racial abuse, bullying in the schools, violence in the homes, disdain for women and basic disregard for human life and common decency? The answer is we talk a great deal about the importance of inter-faith dialogue and ecumenism but such conceptual talk seems to falter when it is applied in practice. I also suspect inter-faith dialogue either takes place at a level way above the common man or is seen in the occasional joint worship at a very local level when the clergy and choirs of different faiths gather for carefully scripted joint worship. I applaud all these initiatives but I am not concerned that one person is a Sikh or a Muslim or a Christian or, indeed, nothing at all. There is room for all the music and all the prayers so long as there is a feeling of goodwill to our neighbours. Academic discussion about the finer points of dogma is fine for academics – in the end of course we will all just have to wait and see!

But let us quickly review some of the religions and faiths. There is not enough room in these few pages to consider every religion but we can look at the main ones as they affect both the UK and India and examine briefly what the different faiths have to offer.

Hinduism is not strictly a religion but it has roughly 700 million followers. It is based on the practice of Dharma, which amounts to a code of life – how to behave in other words. Hinduism has no single founder but Sri Krishnan is the most venerated figure in the Hindu tradition and the Janamashtami festival marks his birth. Hindus believe that the soul passes through a cycle of successive lives (*samsara*) building up good and bad karma along the way. Its next incarnation is always dependent on how the previous life was lived. Moksha is the end of the birth/death cycle and the ultimate goal or *artha*.

Sikhism was founded some 550 years ago by Guru Nanak Dev and is thought to be the 5th largest religion in the world with approximately 25 million followers worldwide. Sikhism believes religion should be practised by living in the real world, coping with life's problems and equality to mankind. *Guru Granth Sahib* is the holy book of Sikhism. Guru is made up from two words – Gu meaning darkness and Ru meaning light. A Guru is someone who is enlightened. Granth is the Punjabi word for book and Sahib is the Hindi word for master. In a Sikh Temple or Gurdwara, the Granth is placed on a raised platform in the main hall (darbar sahib) and covered by an ornate canopy.

Islam, despite what many have come to understand, is first and foremost a peaceful religion; the word Islam itself means 'submission, peace and salvation.' It is the second largest religion in the world with about a billion followers – over one and a half million of them in Britain. Its followers, Muslims, respect Jesus, Moses and Abraham as prophets and believe that Allah (the Arabic for God) sent his last prophet, Mohammed (peace be upon him is the phrase always used after his name), to bring Islam to the world. His whole purpose, as is written in Islam's Holy Book, the *Quran*, is to bring 'a mercy for all the worlds.' Muslims believe there is only one God. There are five basic tenets or pillars of Islam – declaration of faith, praying five times a day, giving money to charity, fasting and a once in a lifetime pilgrimage to Mecca.

Christianity is the largest religion in the world with well over a billion followers and it is also the largest religion in Britain with 30 million faithful, although only a small number say they are active – about 6 million. Christianity was founded by Jesus Christ, the Son of God, over two thousand years ago in Palestine. He was sent down to earth to save mankind from its sins. The church's teachings are written down in the Old and New Testaments of the Bible. The central teaching is that Jesus, the second person in the Holy Trinity – God the Father, the Son and Holy Spirit – died for mankind and rose again on the third day. The protestant Church of England and the Roman Catholic Church are the two major Christian denominations in Britain

Some argue that the problem with religions is that they were created by man who imposed all sorts of different rules and regulations with the obvious outcome of division and conflict even within a single faith; Christianity alone has seen schisms and breakaway movements; apart from the Roman Catholic Church with its authority coming from the Pope in Rome, there is the Orthodox Eastern Church, Armenian Church, Coptics and Jacobite Church. There was also the Protestant Reformation movement and others.

Latterly we have witnessed strenuous efforts to bring all faiths together in a spirit of ecumenism which, while never being suggested as some sort of integration, at least means an acceptance that many faiths can live together in harmony, each one approaching fulfillment and possible salvation albeit by a different path. There is also enormous effort to accommodate different faiths – where once you might just have a chapel at airports for example there are now special prayer rooms for Muslims.

What seems to be missing is the active involvement of religions in daily life. Religion if it is worth anything does not belong in some allocated time slot on a Sunday or a Friday or even in daily worship in a church, temple or synagogue, but in the way we conduct ourselves when we are out and about in the world, not in the solitude of prayer on our knees, although there is probably always time for silent prayer or meditation.

In Roman Catholicism priests and lay ministers will visit the sick of the parish and administer communion or simply sit with them for a while to provide company and solace. There is nothing like that in the Hindu or Sikh tradition. On the other hand Gurdwaras provide daily food and sustenance to all comers regardless of colour or creed. The Christian churches are invariably locked up for most of the week to protect them from vandalism.

A major step forward in integration could be achieved if people accepted that all faiths were at least focused on a common aim – the salvation of mankind by seeking some sort of enlightenment or understanding. It seems all religions recognized the folly and sinfulness of man and that was the inspiration for their foundation. Sikhism, for example, began after Guru Nanak Dev had travelled far and wide and realised that at every turn there were curbs on man's personality and his opportunity for growth; kings were kings and Shudra remained Shudra, there was not only a division between the lowly and the noble, the rich and the poor but also between man and woman. He found that the basis of love and marriage was pecuniary. In short there was total ignorance of true values. Worse still, Guru Nanak found division among religions; the Muslims were the conquerors and the Hindus were the oppressed. Cultural values were flouted by all; the Shudras were exploited by both the Brahmin and the Muslim, neither of whom were following the true teaching of their faiths. This is why Guru Nanak's first major statement was: *There is no Hindu and no Muslim, so whose path shall I follow? I shall follow the path of God.* And turning to women he instructed that they should have equal status with men.

We do not seem to have made much progress. In 1976 the Race Relations Act was passed in Britain but again it is a law which has been enacted and not one which has achieved its underlying aim – unity among the different races in Britain. But perceptions and the reality of life can differ surprisingly. What if the statistics and the trends are right? The high number of inter-ethnic relationships has led to a big increase in the mixed race population of the UK to such an extent that it has become the fastest growing ethnic group in the country with about 415,000 mixed race people or 10% of the total ethnic minority population. People themselves are becoming blurred at the edges and differences are less easy to identify, so where else can we find common grounds? Religion perhaps – hardly.

Where once we were shouting abuse at each other because of the colour of our skin, we are now turning on religion. Those with extremist views are thrown out of the country for inciting racial hatred; we hear that religious centres are being used as breeding grounds for terrorism. But that is precisely what these attitudes are – extreme – they cannot truly reflect what most right thinking people believe. There is probably an easier target to attack – poverty would be a good start. Instead of emphasising their differences all religions could make a joint coordinated effort to influence opinion to combat the hardship faced in many communities. This is a problem which affects all sections of the population not just blacks and Asians.

Interestingly when the British Government was trying to decide what to do with the Millennium Dome some form of multi-themed centre was established and part of that 'theme park' was what became known as the Faith Zone but arguments went on, not only about who would fund it, but what it should include and even what it should be called. In the end a compromise solution was found but like the Dome itself it proved unsuccessful; the problem when it comes to faith and religion is that everyone is concerned about upsetting another group. Humankind is diverse; we cannot all accept and believe what everyone else believes so again, we should celebrate the difference.

The key word there is compromise. In the end there is always compromise. The only certainty in life is death and the most basic requirement for all peoples is how do we cope with death; to put it bluntly, what do we do with the bodies? The various religions prescribe a multitude of different ways of handling and preparing a dead body for burial or cremation; in some traditions it is important to bury the body on the same day or as near to the same day as practicable.

The reality in the modern world is that undertakers – even those who specialise in say Muslim style funerals – cannot fulfill the needs of the family; some even want their loved ones to be transported home which may be in another country. Or someone may have died violently or suddenly and a post-mortem has to be carried out, this can cause a long delay particularly if there has to be a police inquiry. Reluctantly the bereaved family has to agree with the law of the land. The question is, if we can compromise on such a fundamental matter as death, why do we struggle to accept different clothes, religions and other customs?

The answer, of course, is where we can choose we do and that is where artificial distinctions and differences are introduced. When we can afford to choose, or to put it another way when we can afford to discriminate, we do. Look at the people in the slums of the world, their priority is survival. They do not care what someone is wearing, or whether they are praying at the right time of day, or even whether they are praying at all. Their only concern is food and water. This is one of the three basic requirements of humankind – eating, sleeping and reproducing. This is the starting point, the rest is surely vanity or artificial human constraints.

If you have a car why do you need a bigger, newer or faster car or even two cars? If you have a watch why do you need a more expensive watch, it will still only tell you the time of day. But it is not just telling the time of day it is also a statement – I can afford an expensive watch and fine clothes and a big house, therefore I am successful, therefore I am an attractive person. It is back to our primal instincts – if we look attractive we are more likely to find a mate and be able to reproduce.

All religions preach peace and love and understanding but man is not programmed like that. To achieve such peaks of enlightenment he has to work at it either through prayer or meditation. Alternatively why bother? Let us all do our own thing, climb the greasy pole of ambition, have a family if we want one and finally, after our three score year and ten, die.

It seems that we have developed a slight variation on that theme. We have chosen to live in 'tribes' divided along racial lines and we will work to support those within the tribe. Again this is a very basic instinct and eventually, through natural evolution and selection, one tribe or another will come to dominate in a particular region or country. Inevitably that tribe too will start to fragment as internal pressures develop from below and those at the bottom of the pile try to exert their own strength and authority. We can never be satisfied.

This may be our lot – the law of the jungle. From time to time individuals may cross over into an adjoining tribe – the mixed marriages – and gradually over time we will change in looks, in practices and in behaviour. If climate change affects Britain in the way science has predicted, we will become a much warmer country and so the way we dress will have to adapt in the same way as the plants and animals will adapt.

The role of churches and religions, it seems to me, is to help people cope with that existence and make sense of it. Everyone must hope that they will search for elements which bring them closer together, not further apart. I understand that when Pope Benedict XVI reasserted the universal primacy of the Roman Catholic Church in July 2007, approving a document that said Orthodox churches were defective and that other Christian denominations were not true churches, his intention was to clarify what were said to be erroneous interpretations at the Second Vatican Council in the sixties. I suspect the faithful on both sides moved a little further apart when this particular clarification was made.

We will go on searching for the meaning of life without coming to any conclusion – that is our fate. What is interesting to note though is that deeply religious people of all faiths seem to achieve an extraordinary state of contentment which appears to shine out from their faces. Invariably they have very few possessions and ask for nothing. The rest of us will continue chasing that elusive pot of gold at the end of the rainbow which magically will make our lives so much happier. It is just a dream.

As Eknath Easwaran said in his book *The End of Sorrow*: *When we cease to pursue sensory pleasure in the hope of finding lasting joy, which the senses will never be able to give, we come to what the Catho-*

lic mystics call *'holy indifference.'* *This is not a negative state, but a very positive one in which we learn to make the mind undisturbed and equal under all circumstances.*

Some may say this is all very nice and friendly but why bother? The answer is no more complicated than we do it to achieve contentment. We feel we need an extra helping of chocolate ice cream because it tastes so good and we are certain our stomachs can take a little more. But then shortly afterwards, when the pain starts, we realise we have overdone it. Yes, we enjoyed it while we were eating it but the pleasure was only transitory and now we are paying the price. Somehow, we convince ourselves, it will be better next time, but it never is; we assuage what we see as the agony of hunger and we over-indulge, by being greedy about wanting more food, more land, another people's country even, but then the problems start again.

You can take the French writer, Albert Camus's view of the absurdity of it all as depicted in his short essay, *The Myth of Sisyphus*. The dissolute king of Corinth is condemned by the gods to push a boulder up a hill only for it to keep rolling to the bottom again. Camus shows Sisyphus trudging back down again to repeat his mindless task and concludes that the only way he can overcome his punishment is to accept it. Camus tells us we must see Sisyphus as a happy man.

Just look at the arms' race. We all needed bigger and more powerful inter-continental ballistic missiles – purely for protection, of course. Then there was *'glasnost'* and the collapse of the Soviet Union, which ceased to be a threat. Then other nations started to build nuclear weapons, so today Britain feels it needs a nuclear shield, but that upsets the Russians and the merry-go round keeps turning. There will always be buyers for weapons which they will turn on some perceived threat. Millions of dollars will change hands in payment and bribes, but what will change?

Chapter Eleven

The political equation

It is time to engage in a new and honest debate about integration and cohesion in the UK...the context of today's society arguably poses some of the most complex questions we have faced as a nation. With these words, Ruth Kelly, then the Communities Secretary announced a special commission on integration and cohesion in the summer of 2006. One year later the commission delivered its report saying in its opening comments that the *'mood of pessimism that some hold is unjustified'* and that media coverage about 'residential segregation' was excessive. The report stated: *We are a country of many backgrounds and many talents, and to create tomorrow's future today we all need to commit to integration and cohesion being everyone's business.* We certainly do, but the reality is we are not an integrated society. We are a grouping of different communities who, if you like, trade together but seldom live together.

The commission's emphasis was on finding local solutions but it could have gone further and said that the solution rested with individuals. The sad reality is revealed in the endless letters of despair that I have received; it is so often in the families where the attitudes are formed and the trouble arises. The older generations – black and white – are resistant to change and the suspicions kindled by memories of racism and abuse are quick to flare up.

The younger generations are anxious to explore the only world they know, the West, free of social, ethnic and cultural bonds and yet they are essentially cut from the same cloth as their parents. There is no doubt that the better educated and, it has to be said, more affluent, Asians have become totally cosmopolitan and move effortlessly and with ease in any sophisticated company, but the problem lies with the majority who are on the fringes; the ones who have not 'made it' and are never likely to break out of their surroundings to become internationally minded. Rather than thinking locally and acting globally, in the increasingly popular phrase, they are local and will always remain local.

Politicians have to address this sub-culture in the ethnic minority just as much as they have to focus on the marginalised and 'forgotten'. The children and young people in these Asian communities are the ones who look with envious eyes on the opportunities and riches of the Western world and cannot enjoy them and, worse, their parents still have a strong traditional control. They do not move in the fast lane, are not articulate or polished, they remain trapped in an ancient world. These are the girls who find themselves in unloving arranged marriages; these are the sons who behave boorishly towards their wives, suspecting them of being unfaithful, restricting them to a life of tedium and domesticity verging on slavery.

However, rather than dwell on what politicians and governments can and should do to help the situation, we could also focus on matters closer to home for MPs – what is happening in the Houses of Parliament. Fifty years or more of large scale immigration by some highly intelligent people has scarcely been reflected in the make up of the Front Benches. From time to time members of ethnic minorities get appointments to minor government positions or even to the House of Lords – the chairman of the Commission was Darra Singh OBE – but there appears to be a glass ceiling when it comes to the top jobs. There is no specific evidence to support such an assertion but the almost total absence of a black or coloured face at Prime Minister's Question Time every week in the House of Commons is testimony enough; even Prince Charles commented after watching the Trooping the Colour ceremony one year that there were few if any coloured faces among the soldiers on parade.

At a local political level it is a different story where there are many Asian local councillors and officials, but that is hardly surprising if, in some cases, the electorate is predominantly non-white. The trick is to make the leap from local to national prominence and that is a stunt too far, not because people would not have the intelligence to hold down the job, but because it would still be regarded as highly unusual to have a black, Asian or other ethnic minority secretary of state, let alone Prime Minister.

Politics is a game all sides play. Any ethnic minority, including the Asians, delight in inviting MPs, ministers of state or better to their functions and, it has to be said, it is good for politicians to be seen at these functions. At election times, the party bus goes on the road and local MPs lobby hard for the most senior party figure possible to join them. No-one pays too much attention to what is said, just being there is what counts.

Make no mistake, Asians are perfectly capable of playing this game too for their own ends; it looks good to have a recognisable face in the photo-opportunity and that photo is always on display in the office or even in the home. For the Asian it is gamesmanship, putting one over on the neighbour or business contacts and clients. It is all about ego and status and everyone realises the game being played because for the Asian it is just business; socialising is business, holidaying is business.

For the politicians it is all about winning votes and these days there is an important ethnic vote to be captured. There is a certain familiarity about all the speeches at all the dinners and awards ceremonies where token white guests doff their caps to the audience: *We applaud the contribution of the Asian people and welcome them wholeheartedly as fellow citizens as they play such an important part in the success of the economy...etc., etc.,* And that is true, Asians do play a major role in the British economy but after the party, when the speeches are over and the toasts have been made, the cars head off back to their own part of town.

If politicians are to achieve anything in the struggle for true integration they must reach right into the homes and really understand the lives of the Asian people. This means more than rubbing shoulders at glittering events at five star hotels, it means more than inviting the high and mighty for a lunch in the House of Lords and it even means more than just meeting the community leaders many of whom are often accused of being self-appointed spokesmen. They need to visit the Asian strongholds where white people fear to tread at night without a media entourage in tow and without turning it into a photo-opportunity. That is where they will discover the anxieties and aspirations of the people.

It may already be too late to try and immerse Asian people into traditional British society; they came with an open mind but found the obstacles too great so they by-passed them, and now they have by-passed British society altogether. It is an irrelevance to them. The British are surplus to requirements. One young Asian entrepreneur building his business said he was happy to take on all comers as members of staff but of all the people he took on it was the white British who were the least satisfactory and he let them go. The problem was they were not prepared to work overtime whereas the Asians, Poles, Bulgarians and other immigrants were. It seems the Brits were worried about earning too much and that would have meant coming off social security benefits. This is obviously not true of all the unemployed but it is illustrative of the work ethic which is entirely alien to the Asian culture. Taking a horse to water springs to mind – whereas the new arrivals to the UK were ready and able to drink deeply, at least some of the British are not so ready to take advantage of opportunities presented to them. They have no desire to escape from the comfortable restraints of a life on benefits and build for themselves a better existence.

One thing is for certain, the political landscape of Britain will change just as certainly as the economic landscape has already changed for the very simple reason, you cannot keep a good man down. Gradually the Asian 'ghettos' will expand and prosper, the residents will look for new, more up market neighbourhoods and through sheer force of intellect and application they will come to dominate those areas of society and, in time, they will land the more senior political positions. The most obvious effect will be a more cosmopolitan look to the Front Benches, but the more subtle impact will be a broader understanding of ethnic issues which one can safely predict will be near the top of every political agenda along with the environment.

So if there is a glass ceiling preventing Asians from reaching senior positions in government, or for that matter in any other walk of life, it cannot be long before the glass is broken. But in the meantime those in authority should be aware of the pressures each and every new immigrant to this country faces. As Europe grows so will the new arrivals of different ethnic origins – some will view them as a benefit to the British economy, others will see them as a burden to a welfare and housing system already stretched to breaking point.

Are the British basically racist? Some undoubtedly are. The late Bernard Manning, a comedian, openly admitted to being racist and, although his line in comedy was regarded as too offensive for television in the 21st century, he still managed to pack the northern clubs. And yet, while Bernard Manning was not so discreetly removed from the public spotlight, the government chose to honour Salman Rushdie with a knighthood in the 2007 Queen's Birthday Honours for his contribution to literature. The announcement immediately provoked outrage among the worldwide Muslim community who said that the government was effectively honouring a man who had offended their faith with the publication of his book, *The Satanic Verses* in 1988. The former Iranian leader, Ayatollah Ruhollah Khomeini, had issued a 'fatwa' death threat against Rushdie, forcing him into hiding for nearly a decade. There were formal diplomatic protests in Pakistan and Iran as well as public demonstrations. The then Home Secretary, John Reid, immediately hit back saying free speech was of *'overriding political value'* and the former Foreign Secretary, Margaret Becket, told a news conference that the award was *'part of the pattern, that people who are members of the Muslim faith are very much part of our whole, wider community ... and they receive honours in this country in just the same way as any other citizen.'*

Neither Reid nor Beckett would say they are anti-immigrant but it is noticeable that it is increasingly acceptable for politicians to stand up for the indigenous British population in the face of growing immigration. While still Chancellor of Exchequer, Gordon Brown was suggesting that British jobs should go to Britons. This was not regarded as being racist and nor was the call, mentioned previously, that we should have a Britain Day. But the very fact that politicians dare to suggest such things is perhaps indicative of a new mood swing. Do politicians detect that the ethnic white Briton has had enough of the multicultural changes that are taking place? Or is it fear of what might happen if the problem is not addressed? Growing up is hard enough to do, growing up a stranger in a foreign land is even harder, growing up in a country where you feel you belong and yet somehow believe you are regarded by the majority as an alien is the hardest of all.

Britons are instinctively reluctant to mix, it is their inbred reserve. They find it hard to get along with each other let alone a 'foreigner'. In June 2007 as the Prime Minister, Tony Blair, was preparing to hand over power to Gordon Brown, the whole Europe question loomed again. Most of the population, if we were to believe the opinion polls, wanted a referendum on Europe and, if one were held, most we were told would vote to pull out; we do not like being told what to do by Europe and increasingly Europe was being opened up to people and nations with which we had nothing in common.

But you cannot put the genie back in the box. Britain is already a multiracial, multicultural, multi-faith society. The problem for the politicians as they make the laws and for us as citizens as we have to find a way of getting along is how do we convince ourselves that beneath the skin we are all essentially doing the same thing – trying to survive. If we return to the report by the commission on integration and cohesion, they rightly placed an emphasis on a common language – English. Instead of providing translators and multi-language signs, the emphasis, the report recommended, should be on language training. In other words the first step should be to understand each other. The next step will be harder – to try and understand the history, culture, style, habits and the very nature of each other.

There was a television programme recently called 'Why Birds Sing'. There were two arguments – the artists felt the birds enjoyed their songs while the scientists said it was simply a survival instinct – by making the most beautiful sounds the birds attracted mates, much as peacocks have extravagantly coloured tails for no other purpose than to look attractive. We could draw our own lesson from this by first enjoying and appreciating the interesting differences between races and then take it a step further and try to understand why people are as they are. The Indian word, *samabuddhi,* meaning 'having an equal attitude towards all' is a target worth aiming for. Politicians being politicians will 'go with the flow'; they want to be elected above all else. It is probably up to people to take the lead in going that extra mile towards real understanding of all our neighbours.

A last thought on politics is apathy. Not only do we not vote in elections – only 59.4% bothered to turn out in the 2001 general election, the lowest figure since 1918, but we are simply not taking part in life. We are not unique in this respect. Professor Robert Putnam in his book, *Bowling Alone,* noted that fewer Americans were taking part in civic activities. He took bowling as an example. While the numbers of people bowling in the US had increased the numbers of those participating in leagues had actually decreased. So to have fun people were bowling alone. In the same way people were able to see more of the world around them but they did that by watching television, further isolating themselves from the community.

With the immigration temperature rising in the UK, Putnam was interviewed again on BBC Radio in June 2007. He said that as communities became more diverse they tended to trust each other less, not only from race to race but even within their own race. A common language was important but he thought it was important to set that language teaching in a community context so the participants had more than just the language in common; they could be members of a club for example where not only did they learn English but they had a secondary common interest such as football.

Membership of any local committee or council is low and public attendance minimal or non-existent. Few have time these days to step outside their homes and participate in the running of even their local village. In any club it is always the same, a few stalwarts who run the shows. Multiply that up to a city like London where there is a general sense of nervousness about crime and once we are inside, the doors are locked and we remain cocooned in our own worlds until it is time for work the next day.

If we choose not to participate then we cannot be heard. The few who are prepared to attend the meetings, go on the hustings and tramp the streets in search of votes will be elected by default. As the Electoral Commission set up to oversee the elections in 2001 said, voter apathy raises questions of legitimacy at the heart of democracy.

If we are to trust each other, even our 'own kind', we have got to talk to them.

Chapter Twelve

The bottom line is money

We are not so different when it comes to work – we all want to make money and we probably do not care too much who the customers are. What we do care a great deal about is whom we will allow into our business; the business partners and colleagues. Just as they like to live in their own communities, Asians tend to hunt together when it comes to business. Just skirt round Heathrow off the M4 and you will find the Asian traders hard at work in West London, employing fellow Asians, continue round to North and East London and there are more enclaves. It is convenient, near their homes and nothing is wasted in grand buildings. Apart from the offices and the temperature these pockets could easily be India judging by the majority population. They are happy to take on the premises which others have rejected. From time to time the buildings are either extended or the business expands to such an extent that new premises are required, but still they remain close by, close to their roots you might even say.

The focus is always on the bottom line, keeping overheads down, no wastage on prestigious addresses, fancy carpets, lighting or design, just get the raw materials in and ship out the product. Even in a casual conversation Asians will quickly get down to the profitability about any enterprise dismissing anything which cannot at least become a big business as not worth pursuing. More, big, international, growth – these are the key words. And all these will lead to new wealth and prosperity for the owners and their families. There is never any room for outsiders or so it appears. As the founding father gets older the sons assume more responsibility and if there are no sons, the nephews. It remains in the family, which is fair and wise enough but it perpetuates the isolation. The common language spoken in many businesses is not English but one of the Indian based languages; the letters and computer communications are, of course, in English but the 'shop-floor' is pure Indian. The English job-seekers, even if they knew of a vacancy and there never seem to be any, would not survive. They would not like the long hours, the culture or even understand what their colleagues were saying.

Even some major companies are effectively Little Indias – the receptionist is Indian, the entire accounting department is likely to be Indian and all administration is probably Indian. The only time you might see a white face is when drivers make pick-ups or deliveries. There are big family enterprises where only the male members of the family are taken on leaving the females to bring up the children. So not only is there a mild form of racism being practised – Asians only – there is also a seriously non-PC attitude to women's rights, but this is the reality of Asian business. No-one raises objections or lobbies their union representative even if one existed, they all just accept that this is the way Asians do business, it works in India and Pakistan and it will work in the UK.

New migrants can mean new growth for the British economy but with the new wealth comes new burdens. David Frost, Director General of the British Chambers of Commerce, said: *(It) is right to say that UK businesses have benefited enormously from the recent high levels of migration yet it has to be recognised that this has brought with it enormous social consequences... . Skilled, work-hungry migrants are masking the tragic lack of skills so many of our school leavers have. A generation is in danger of going from school straight to welfare with no experience of work and the Government must recognise the danger that this presents."*

Asians have been used to a culture of self-reliance and mutual support within their own community. In the same way more recently the influx of Polish citizens have quickly established their own sectors, businesses, cafes and food-outlets offering a home from home service of typical Polish delights. It is natural for their businesses to be established in their own area and to expand from there; they have friends and family and they have customers who speak their own language. Why should they try and move into unfriendly, or at least, unfamiliar territory? There are some notable exceptions which prove the rule, those which transcend cultures – foods, beers, technology – but even if the corporate head office moves to more prestigious quarters in the centre of a town or city, the real production work takes place out in the suburbs.

The traditional Asian businesses are the rag trade, IT and cars or the professions – banking, doctors and lawyers. It is rare for children even to be allowed to venture off into something more creative like the arts. But the Bollywood mood has captured the world's imagination, Asian actors and actresses have crossed the cultural divide and TV and radio stations have sprung up to cater for their captive audience of non-English speakers waiting at home; providing some comfort for sure but adding to the feeling of isolation without doubt.

Some say that much of the Asian work is simply cheap copying and Britain is encouraging it. The rag trade only requires someone with an alert eye to fly to India, note the styles and colours being ordered by the fashion buyers from New York, France and London and simply produce a cheap copy. That may well be so, but it is a business and like all Asian business the owners will always be prepared to work hard at it often turning a single shop into a thriving empire.

Life is business for the Asian; there is no such thing as time off, the pursuit of pleasure just for the sake of it. Every party or meal is a potential deal. The value and importance of success and worldly possessions is the driver. Religious pictures are always on prominent display in Asian offices or homes but what makes everyone happy is money. The relentless pursuit of profit, the big deal regardless of whether or not it is at someone else's expense. But these are transitory. Sri Krishna teaches in the Gita:

> *'... we experience cold or heat, pleasure or pain.*
> *These are fleeting: they come and go.*
> *Bear them patiently...'*

Gandhi put it another way when he saw a lady bedecked in fine jewels: *Your beauty does not depend on diamonds; your beauty comes from inside.* It is the norm in Asian social circles for the women to wear their finest clothes and jewels – ostentation is acceptable, even obligatory. Everyone is constantly assessing what the other guests are wearing, where did they go on holiday, how often, which car are they driving or how their children are getting on in school. The concept on one upmanship is not seen as an impolite way of behaving rather as a statement of success.

It seems at every turn we are all different – the way we work and play. Envy, a universal vice, either spurs people into action to match and exceed what their neighbours have or turns to resentment and anger. Mothers want their daughters to marry well, improve on what they themselves have, so they push hard to find the right husbands; they want to know what line of business they are in and ideally how much is in their bank accounts. It is instinctive, a matter of self-preservation as well – a good son-in-law means they will be well cared for in their old age.

For so many Asians who arrived in the UK in the sixties they were poor, but poverty was not a trap, it was an incentive to succeed. In another of their harrowing reports, the Joseph Rowntree Foundation found that white British pupils from low income families not only form the majority of low educational achievers; they also do worse than children with similar income levels from other ethnic groups. Predictably Chinese and Indian pupils are most likely to succeed.

What will be the real division between people in years to come in the UK? Will it be the colour of their skin or their creed or will it simply come down to money? Asians will go on working hard and will enjoy the luxury lifestyle that the West has to offer; other immigrants escaping poverty in Eastern Europe will continue to flock to the Promised Land where so much help is offered free; who could resist? But not all immigrants become the star turn of the corporate sector. Money attracts money and those with opportunity, connections and family wealth will prosper while at the other end of the scale there will be many who remain in their secluded, segregated communities. All these successful companies still rely on the workers to pack and unpack the boxes, stack the shelves, attach the widgets.

Agony aunts see the underside of life, the worries, hardships, loneliness, the drinking and the misery. Do not be fooled by the ostentation and the wealth, all these troubles can be found just as easily in the glamorous homes with gilt furnishings and marble as they can in the long drab lines of terraced housing. There are jealousies, affairs and divorce, there is bullying and beating, the only difference is that with wealth it is easier to escape and move on. Philandering, or to give it its real name, cheating on one's partner, is as commonplace in Asian society as it is in British society; as in both groups if you have money you seem to be able to get away with it. It is common for the very rich to marry and divorce on numerous occasions, the stigma which it once attracted in Asian families is no more among the affluent.

But the troubles Britain will face if it does not find a workable solution to the dislocated ethnic groups will not come from the comfortably rich, it will come from the disgruntled who may have 'proper professional' jobs, such as doctors, and from the underclass who have not succeeded. Many of them will be second or third generation Brits who feel they are not really accepted or are angered by every perceived insult real or imagined.

The business community, and that includes the Asian businesses, have a role to play in finding the answers along with the local and national government. But the truth of the matter is they will not find time. Picture the scene in a cramped, noisy textile business on the outskirts of London. Boxes are being prepared, shipments are moving in and out, meetings are being held and phone calls being made. This activity continues probably six or even seven days a week. Who in this situation is going to give a moment's thought to what their staff are doing when they are not at work? Who will be bothered whether or not their employees' children are progressing at school, integrating with others, joining clubs? No one. Instead the workers will make their weary way back home by public transport and lock the door firmly behind them not for one moment having either wanted or been able to brush with the British community.

This is not integration, it is survival. But then what happens? The man running the local corner shop starts expanding; along with his van which he uses to stock up from the cash and carry, he now drives a bigger car. Then the envy kicks in and the local lads, who have probably made life difficult for the shopkeeper, run their keys along the paintwork. It will not take much to spark trouble but it will come from long, simmering resentment. Someone will put a religious spin on it but that will not be the underlying cause. Real Muslims, Christians and Hindus are perfectly capable of sitting down to a meal together or to doing a business deal together; they are also perfectly happy for the others to follow their own belief. Unrest when it happens, and it will, comes from the most basic and basest of human emotions – jealousy, anger, frustration, fear.

So we return to our theme the myth of UK integration and when it comes to business, as it is in how we live and how we pray, we are no more integrated than if the businesses were being conducted in India or Pakistan. Occasionally you have a high flyer – usually in the world of finance – who breaks through the glass ceiling and makes it on to the board or even becomes chief executive but they are noticeable precisely because they are exceptional. Does it matter if the economy is booming and jobs are being created? Or is it the 'Bowling Alone' syndrome identified by Professor Putnam? We are all just getting on with our lives, 'doing our own thing' and we would really prefer not to talk to our neighbours. It is actually beginning to sound very British. The worry is that this is not just a case of individuals keeping themselves to themselves, it is whole communities and those communities will become whole cities, e.g. Leicester. Is it really acceptable for vast tracts of Britain to be dominated by a single race? Inevitably such communities work for the good of themselves not the country as a whole. This is hardly the 'cohesion' the Government is seeking to achieve, if by cohesion we mean sticking together, and it is clearly not integration.

If we do not think of ourselves as English, British, Asian or Anglo-Asian perhaps the best hope is to define ourselves as being from a particular town or even finding 'solidarity' and unity by being part of a club. Curiously the football match is an example where, for a couple of hours, people of different backgrounds come together; they cheer on their team which might be a club side or say the England team. Black, white, Christian and Muslim will all shout in unison as their side scores a goal. Do they think of themselves as English, Asian, British, Scottish? No, they define themselves as Chelsea or Arsenal supporters and, as one young businessman, building up his own company, said he thought of himself as a Londoner, born and bred. He had lived all his life in London and that was who he was. He was as clear about that as he was about the business he had started from scratch and was growing rapidly.

Curiously this takes us back to the structure of Indian society. When the warlike Aryans swept down through the Indus Valley in the second millennium BC they did not build cities but they organised themselves in tribal units called *Jana*. As they spread across India the *Jana* soon became the basic social structure which in time became geographical becoming known as *jana-rajyapada* or national kingdom. Such was the loyalty to these sub-units that even to this day Indians define themselves as being from these territorial regions which all have their separate cultures, styles of dress, language and food.

Maybe we in Britain can learn something from that form of division. First identify with your local community, get involved in its activities. It could certainly help many who struggle to know who they really are – torn between an Asian culture which is alien to them and yet made to feel uncomfortable in the only land they have ever known. They can be inspired by the opening lines to the composer Hubert Gregg's famous song popularized by Budd Flanagan in 1944 – *'Maybe it's because I'm a Londoner, that I love London so.'*

Chapter Thirteen

Media – friend or foe?

Sometimes it is hard to remember that as recently as 1945, communications were relatively basic. We had wireless and newspapers, television was improving but it was something of a luxury in most homes. For Indians living in the UK far from home these were anxious times as their homeland was struggling for independence. There was rioting between Muslims and Hindus which became more intense as 1947 approached. The only source of regular and up to date information was the radio. People were worried about their families, were they alive or dead? The British on the other hand who had been in India in the high days of the Raj had enjoyed the experience; they were waited on hand and foot, life was truly luxurious, while at home there were only the privations of war, there was debris, destruction and rationing. In those days the media – radio and newspapers – were definitely regarded as a friend, even a lifeline, albeit an extended and sometimes fractured lifeline. Today it is instantaneous, comprehensive, impressive and, at times, destructive.

Our news priorities have also been skewed in favour of the celebrity. The most talked about alleged act of racism in Britain in early 2007 was against the Indian actress, Shilpa Shetty, by fellow housemates on Channel Four television's 'Celebrity Big Brother'. In the end Shilpa Shetty won the competition and she was feted by one and all, including a visit to the Houses of Parliament with plenty of media coverage.

Abuse of anyone's colour or religion is unacceptable in any civilized community if for no other reason than it is bad man-

ners. It does not need to be taken any further; one should not
be rude to people or about people for whatever reason. But what
was the Shilpa Shetty affair really all about? In the great scheme
of things it was a game show which people entered precisely to
gain publicity, revive fading status or to achieve that elusive 15
minutes of fame. It certainly helped raised the international
profile of a Bollywood actress who perhaps was not in the 'A'
list and all credit to her for taking full advantage of the opportunity. It also helped the ratings for a TV show. But did we all
lose our sense of perspective? Gordon Brown, then Chancellor
of the Exchequer, had to interrupt more urgent matters on a
trip to India to defend Britain against charges of racism. It was
headline news on Indian TV, in the city of Patna effigies of the
housemates were burnt, and Keith Vaz MP raised the matter in
the British Parliament.

Anyone who dares to mention the word race or even religion
is in danger of offending someone; are people terrorists or freedom fighters is the classic question. Jomo Kenyatta was a terrorist until, under the guidance of Britain, following a spell in
prison, he blossomed into Kenya's President. Is there such a
place as Palestine or should one refer to the Palestinian Territo-
ries? Should we ever criticise preachers in a mosque regardless
of what they say?

The French have no qualms about such matters, they throw
radical imams out of the country without a moment's hesitation, the police are allowed to walk into any mosque and the
majority support the government ban on the wearing of the *hijab*
in schools. And in 2010 France's lower parliament voted over-
whelmingly for an outright ban on wearing the full veil in public. The British government has been altogether more cautious,
anxious not to offend or curtail freedom of speech. But there
are signs of a hardening of attitude.

While he was still Home Secretary, John Reid, said, *'I want
to change that culture so we can have that mature discussion.'* He

went on, 'We have to get away from this daft so-called politically correct notion that anybody who wants to talk about immigration is somehow a racist. That isn't the case.'

And leading Muslims in the British community, like Lord Noon, chairman of Noon Group, urged the Labour Government, to follow the French lead and get tough on terror. Writing in the *Financial Times*, he said, *'Liberality has been misused by radical imams to sow the seeds of hatred in young minds and send them out to perpetrate acts of violence.'* He went on, *'Much more needs to be done to stamp out violence in the name of Islam.'*

This was echoed by the secretary general of the Muslim Council of Britain, Dr Muhammad Abdul Bari, who was quoted as saying, *'These people who attempt to kill or maim in this way are enemies of us all. The police and security services have the enormous responsibility for trying to ensure the safety of all Britons. As such they deserve the fullest support and co-operation from each and every sector of society, including Muslims.'*

The challenge for the media is to be able to report the facts as they see them without being accused of whipping up a frenzy of emotion and, just as importantly, without being afraid to report things as they are. The failed car bomb attacks in London and Glasgow in July 2007 prompted comment columns in the media such as this one in the *Evening Standard* by Nick Cohen under the headline: 'These days I'm proud to be called intolerant.' He wrote: *'Along with a small band of like-minded souls, I've been battering at the comforting notion that you can explain radical Islam as a natural reaction against British foreign policy. All right, we say, our leaders are not always wise or good. But to pretend that a global psychopathic movement inspired in equal measure by religious fanaticism and Nazi conspiracy theory is a rational response to Western provocation is to engage in wishful thinking on an epic scale.'*

The way the media report events will always provoke criticism; it is a truism that if one knows anything about a story one will find a mistake. Even the focus of coverage can come in for criticism. The Metropolitan Police Chief at the time, Sir Ian Blair, accused the media of 'institutional racism' in its reporting of murders. He was reacting angrily to suggestions that the police did not give equal resources to crimes against white people and ethnic minorities. He said that the resources were the same, the difference was how they were reported by the media, *'I actually believe that the media is guilty of institutional racism in the way they report deaths.'* Referring to the murder of a white lawyer he said, *'That death of the young lawyer was terrible, but an Asian man was dragged to his death, a woman was chopped up in Lewisham, a chap shot in the head in a Trident murder – they got a paragraph.'*

But it was ever thus. It is not being xenophobic if one reports a plane crash and says, 'Two Britons were among the 180 dead...' or if the story of an earthquake is put lower down the running order of a programme than say a multiple motorway crash in the UK in which perhaps 'only' one or two people died. Viewers and readers are getting what the editors believe they want; if the papers are sold and the viewers keep watching nothing will change. On American television it was difficult to find any international coverage before the arrival of the likes of CNN. It is too easy to criticise the media for their coverage of events, all sorts of hidden factors come into play when preparing say a TV news programme. Crucially there must be pictures and if the footage is good the story will move up the running order or bump another perhaps more interesting, even more important, story without pictures off the programme altogether. TV news is showbiz, presentation, why else would the presenters walk about the set as they introduce the next item rather than sitting still behind a desk. There was a time when adjectives were forbidden in the presenter's script, now the 'intros' are part of the drama.

It is perfectly plain to everyone that immigration has increased dramatically but it does not affect every community equally, the south-east inevitably bears the largest burden. At the same time it would be fair to say that the south-east also enjoys the benefits. The immigrants have to be housed, watered and fed, their children have to be educated and the health needs cared for, but so too have the needs of the indigenous population. Cheap labour means fewer jobs for the existing unemployed at least some of whom would prefer to remain on welfare benefits quite simply because it is more lucrative.

So much for the reporting of economics. The media should be just as candid and frank when it comes to reporting the impact of religious fervour in the country. Islam believes there is only one true faith and all non-believers are infidel. The Roman Catholics also pray that everyone converts to Catholicism. Both are perfectly acceptable but neither can be allowed to exert undue influence or worse issue and carry out threats of violence. While staunchly defending everyone's right to freedom of speech, no-one should condone incitement to hatred or murder.

The problem with the immigration debate is that it very soon moves from economics to religion and often with an injection of politics. As the temperature rises, lucid thinking evaporates and it is not long before matters degenerate into out and out racism and abuse. You might say if it just remained at the level of name calling we could manage but in the current climate it soon turns to violence.

The role of the media is surely to portray the facts and to inform, whether by debate or drama. It comes back to learning about each other. There is no room for extremism but communities should manage their own and control the excesses of speech and behaviour. If necessary they should disown the hotheads and identify them to the authorities but that requires a level of trust which for the most part does not exist today.

The question is to what extent is the media getting through to its target audience? Visit many Asian households and you will find Asian newspapers and magazines in Guajarati, Bengali and Punjabi and invariably the TV will be showing Asian language programmes; even the media which is in English is targeted at the Asian audience. Anything that is written or said does not reach the indigenous British population; the comments, editorials and letters may well be full of sound comment but the audience is restricted. In the same way much of the English language output may well not percolate through to the Asian population.

In short there is no cross-fertilisation of ideas, thoughts, humour or opinions and it is even perpetuating divisions between Indians reflecting the divisions of race and creed back in India. So deep-rooted is the division and mistrust that even when a car bursts into flames at the entrance to Glasgow airport or bombs fail to go off in London and educated men and women are arrested in international swoops, the suspicion among some Asians is that the whole story has somehow been fabricated in an elaborate conspiracy by the authorities in collusion with the media.

Once again it is as though there are parallel worlds out there; everyone goes shopping in the same town but probably frequents different shops. We move and breathe in the same space but the non-Asian or non-white residents are effectively invisible to one another. Try saying good morning to someone as you pass on the pavement and see the look of astonishment on their faces. It will be a mixture of surprise, delight and suspicion and all you will have done is acknowledged their existence.

The theatre, cinema and television all have such an important part to play in introducing to the rest of the community the different world in which ethnic minorities live; the likes of 'Bend It Like Beckham' or the successful play, 'Rafta Rafta', by Ayub Khan-Din, which was an adaptation of the comedy 'All in Good Time' by Bill Naughton replacing the northern family with an Asian family, all help to open our eyes to what has become of 'our' country and our fellow citizens.

But while the playwrights and film directors do their bit, the news media so often remain focused on the bad news; good news we know from experience does not sell newspapers – people have tried and failed – we want the anger, the violence and the mayhem. However, we should remember that we are not idle spectators, this is our community in turmoil. We are one community, after all the UK is not a big country. While we continue to skirt round the issues, turn away when we do not like the look of our neighbours, we will have conflict. Lord Powell of Bayswater, private secretary to Margaret Thatcher, said that she did not spend much time in her Dulwich home because it meant driving through Brixton which she disliked. She was fortunate in that she was able to move home, but we all do it, side-step awkward situations, avoid confrontation and maybe hope the problem will go away. It will not, of course, and if we treat immigration as a problem as opposed to an opportunity we will not make progress.

The news media are pack animals. Once a theme has caught the public imagination they will run with it until something new hits the headlines. In the summer of 2007 honour killings in the UK were attracting attention and the links were being made between such extreme behaviour and terrorism. Such stories only serve to prove that right-thinking citizens of every background must work harder to establish, maintain and improve interracial links. The real worry is that when committees and working parties of eminent people are established they operate in a rarefied atmosphere far removed from the misery in the forgotten and segregated communities. This is where resentment festers and breeds.

You cannot make people get along and you cannot blame the media for reporting terrible stories in a dramatic fashion, but equally we all cannot move to a 'better neighbourhood' and simply ignore the problem. Maybe the best hope is to encourage a sense of belonging to a particular area; take pride in being from

Yorkshire or Wales or London. What is certain is that 'belonging' is a basic human desire. Not many people are loners, most of us since childhood wanted to be part of the gang and to be left out was upsetting and alienating.

Asians, Poles, Kurds and Bulgarians have all come to the UK to better themselves. It is inevitable that they will congregate together to achieve a sense of belonging and to be near their 'own kind'. But that should only be a bridgehead to engage with the rest of British society. Their part of town should not become a ghetto, however prosperous, and nor should it become a no-go area.

The tragedy of the stories about honour killings and the more frequent but seldom reported beatings and virtual imprisonment in their own homes of Asian girls and women is that the victims have, in effect, being trying to reach out to the world beyond their own communities. They may have been attracted to white men or they may only have wished to talk in a civilised fashion with non-Asians with no sexual intention in mind. Muslims, Hindus even Christians have nothing to fear from such encounters. All these faiths are strong enough to allow such interchange. People do have doubts about their faith from time to time – cruelty is no way to preserve a man or a woman's faith. It may be possible to imprison them in their own homes, it may even be possible to force a girl to marry someone against her will, but that cannot bring greater love and acceptance of a faith if it allows such practice.

The media are right to pursue and expose such horror stories and no faith is immune. The Roman Catholic church has been rightly investigated for sexual abuse by priests over the years. Films have been made about the barbaric treatment meted out to young, single girls who became pregnant in Ireland in the past. If the church cannot take the criticism and put its own house in order, what right has any priest to stand up in the pulpit on a Sunday and preach? Equally the Muslim and Hindu faiths have a great history which can stand confidently on their basic tenets; there is no call for, no rule or law which demands, cruelty or ill-treatment. The teachings and scriptures of all faiths are there for interpretation and guidance of the faithful. When the Bible advises us to 'pluck out thine eye if it offends thee' it does not mean you should literally poke out your eye if you look with admiration at a beautiful woman who is not your wife. Something or someone of beauty is 'admirable'. There is a difference between looking and ogling.

Television news can only give a snapshot of any story. Two and a half minutes is regarded as a significant length of time to allocate to an event and coverage of that duration can only be cursory at best. But most people rely entirely on television for all their information making the obligation on the programme editors to achieve balance and honesty all the more important. Despite claims to the contrary, the frantic rush of putting a news programme together does not allow much room for political bias. An honour killing is horrific enough in its basic detail without seeking to inject some anti-faith bias. But it is the way that story is interpreted by the viewer which is important. We should think first about the victim and try and understand the pressures she is under, and then try and understand how a man, a father or brother or uncle, can be driven to such violence.

If communities are left alone they cannot benefit from exchanges of ideas, culture, music, art, history. It is the duty of the media to report and explain and it is the responsibility of the readers and viewers to read and view intelligently. Not all Roman Catholic priests are paedophiles and not all Muslim fathers are capable of murdering their own daughter in the name of honour.

Chapter Fourteen

Old times, new times – plus ça change

The beauty of delving back in time is that so often you discover the unexpected which more often than not has the habit of upsetting strongly-held beliefs and assumptions. It also usually proves that nothing is new. The origins of the Indians are a case in point.

Take the Dravidian people of Southern India. The term Dravidian describes the people and their family of languages – more than 70 variations. Their skin colour can range from very dark to almost white. According to one population geneticist L.L. Cavalli-Sforza of Stanford, working in the 1980s, almost all Indians are genetically Caucasian, or at least far closer to West Europeans than to East Asians. Then you have the Aryans, the nomadic warlike people from the barren Euro-Asian steppes who invaded Northern India. The arrival of the Aryans raised problems both political and racial as we have seen, setting groups of people from the same country apart in the caste system, problems which persist to this day.

Invaders and even immigrants have an impact on any society and they have always done so. If they settle in the country their physical appearance, their habits, culture and their beliefs are bound to influence the host nation.

The United Kingdom is not being invaded – although some might argue the case – but newcomers are arriving from many different parts of the world and they are making an impression. The new arrivals cannot simply pretend the indigenous population does not exist and instead try to build up a country within a country; equally the indigenous population cannot shut their eyes and hope the interlopers will somehow vanish. They won't. Quite obviously both groups have to accommodate each other but the sad part is we are resisting at every turn.

As an agony aunt knows, human nature will prevail in the end – for good or ill. A typical case was of a young girl who had fallen in love with a white man who was working in the same office. Her parents had naturally introduced her to a number of 'suitable' Indian boys but each one was rejected by the girl who had made up her mind. The parents were devastated and in desperation they asked my advice, which meant they wanted their daughter to be told to cooperate with the parents. In a vain attempt to calm the situation both sides of the argument were explored and I urged the parents to think of the positive aspects of a mixed marriage. Neither side would shift their ground. Six months later the girl married her English boyfriend. The parents were mortified.

You cannot fight nature, you cannot resist love but that will not stop people trying. Indians have been in the UK now for half a century and still parents are sticking to the old traditions of a country they either left long ago or maybe even never knew. Why? Remembering traditions and customs even dusting them off from time to time on special days is one thing, being stuck in the past refusing to budge from proudly held customs to the detriment of one's own family is quite another. Nothing can stop the inevitable consequence of two or more peoples mixing and working together. And yet if you asked the young Asian men and women, the vast majority would be in favour of allowing their parents to introduce them to a prospective spouse. British youngsters would be appalled, even embarrassed, by the prospect of parents 'setting up' such a meeting, but some traditions die hard.

In time the very appearance of the 'typical' Anglo-Saxon will change, perhaps becoming a little darker and the fourth and fifth generation people of Asian origin will become a little lighter. Is that such an appalling prospect? White people race off to the sun every holiday to 'top up their tans' while black people do everything to make their hair look straight.

Instinctively it seems we are trying to look like each other, blend with the surroundings and above all not stand out. But it will take time and we must give it time. There are still many Indian, Pakistani, Bangladeshi and Sri Lankan families who are not ready to let go of the old days and move into the new world – a world which they themselves have adopted. They are in denial, you might say, or perhaps it is simply a question of trust. They are afraid to drop their guard having suffered years of racial abuse and they are suspicious of the authorities which they perceive to be on the side of whites. Honour is at stake and when there is no interaction with anyone outside a community traditional ways, long held suspicions and fear are hard to change. It is not just a question of intermarriage, these feelings govern every aspect of life including education and upbringing. The NSPCC recently reported that most Asian families would not report cases of child abuse to the authorities preferring to tackle it themselves because is was a question of *izzat*, family honour, and that came before everything including the suffering of an individual whatever the age.

A characteristic not to be under-estimated in the Indian is pride. Indians are proud of their heritage and culture, proud of their nation and, to a certain extent, the older generation in particular regard the giving up of long held customs as a sort of surrender and demeaning. Some Indians are happy to change, they would regard it as moving with the times and feel free to adopt new ideas, others are not so sure and feel guilty having sacrificed something for the sake of mere convenience. Surrender is anathema to the warrior Sikhs, in particular. They remember their history. Following the Battle of Sabraon in 1846, described by Lord Gough as the 'Waterloo of India' which ended the First Anglo-Sikh War, blame was laid squarely at the feet of the commanders Lal Singh and Tej Singh who fled the battle. The infamy of their cowardice will forever be remembered by Sikhs in the lines translated as:

> *Laloo lost the blush of shame,*
> *Teju lost his lustre,*
> *By turning their backs in the field*
> *They turned the tide and the battle yield.*

The important point for all people to remember is that everyone has their dignity, their pride if you like, and that should be respected, which is not the same as remaining aloof or apart. When Indian husbands lock their wives in their homes, not to protect them but to keep them from perceived temptation that does not preserve dignity it preserves insecurity and suspicion, quite apart from its inhumanity. When parents forbid their daughters from going out with white children for fear that they will fall in love and be tempted by Western ways that does not encourage family trust, it breeds resentment.

Segregation and isolation has been ingrained into the Indian way of life for centuries, the whole social structure of Indian society is an extraordinary contradiction of unity in diversity and rigid demarcation between groups. The Indian community in the UK is managing to preserve the old while adopting the new. The 'untouchables' are thriving in a land where caste distinction is unknown, but among themselves the divisions are strictly preserved. It is perfectly possible, and there are plenty of examples, for the Dalits – oppressed people – to become millionaires in Britain and receive honours from the government. But they will not marry, pray or party with Indians from another caste.

In today's new world where anything is possible – anyone can become a tycoon with the right idea and drive – Asians still rigidly cling to their traditional ways; the most cosmopolitan and 'integrated' do it when it suits them, but for the vast majority the social, business and communications divide remains in tact. In their heart of hearts most indigenous white Britons probably feel the same. There is virtually no exchange of ideas at a local level between different races – Arabs, Chinese, Asians. Little wonder then that moderation, consensus and mutual respect are having no impact. Events in London during the summer of 2007, when highly educated Asians suspected of being involved in the failed bombings were arrested, underlined what police have long known that radical elements can easily be found among the successful and intelligent people. Are we really surprised then when extremists emerge among the dispossessed, the poor and the resentful immigrants? There is no other balancing voice in their lives; they brood and complain about their lot in dingy surroundings and the most susceptible, urged on by the friends and occasionally their 'spiritual' advisers, look for an escape, perhaps even in what they come to believe as heroic martyrdom.

As an agony aunt, one can look back over 50 years of correspondence recounting tales of love and loneliness, misery and mistreatment, joy and sorrow and wonder when people will ever learn. Are things getting better in our multi-cultural society? If one is being optimistic, one would say things at least are evolving. But if one is being a realist, one would say that after half a century of 'living together' we are as divided as ever only now there is the added dimension of religious hatred.

The new world of Britain in the 21ˢᵗ century is, at the very best, a world of suspicion. The English do not readily see a distinction between Hindu and Muslim, so all Indians and Pakistanis are the same. They can see the difference between and Indian and an Arab but not between Arab and say Kurd, Sunni and Shia. The reaction is, they are all a bunch of foreigners who have taken over the country – kick them all out.

It is easy for a Bishop and an Imam to sit down together and discuss the finer points of their religions, seeking ways of moving closer together in a spirit of understanding if not ecumenism.

But it is impossible for the average British citizen to find common ground with the Pakistani family who might be running the corner shop. Their lives are too sharply divided and with each bomb blast or attempted terrorist attack on innocent people in a city centre, the wider the divide becomes. This is not the book to debate the whys and wherefores of such attacks, the rights and wrongs of particular actions, but an agony aunt sees the impact of these events as they ripple down through society. I can also see the tremors moving in the other direction; relatively trivial events of say bullying at school or the occasional racial taunt or insult all too easily escalate into anger and hatred.

Wars happen because people do not talk and the first skirmishes happen at a local, even personal level. Children will not listen to their parents; parents fail to appreciate the desires and aspirations of their children. Add tradition, culture, religion, poverty, envy, jealousy, lust, greed and ego to the mix and it is surprising that we are not permanently at each other's throats. We are not because sense, understanding, tolerance and cooperation provide a soothing balm. Mahatma Gandhi never raised his hand in anger, never fired a shot and had no possessions, and yet his influence on the future path of an entire nation was more powerful than any gun. He was and remains respected by ordinary men and women the world over regardless of their race or creed. His example should shame the world today. Every religion has examples of such powerful simplicity, but most of us never think about them unless we happen to attend our temples, churches, gurdwaras, mosques or synagogues and even then we quickly forget the advice and teachings the moment we leave.

When a frightened, anxious teenage girl writes about her 'forbidden' love for a boy, or a wife calls me in tears about the abuse she is suffering, what advice can I give? You really want to talk to the parents of the girl or the husband of the wife and make them face the challenge – why do you forbid such a marriage after all it is only a girl and a boy in love, make that your starting point not the baggage of family tradition, race or even religion. And why is such violence being meted out by the husband? What is his real concern? Why is he angry or jealous? All should start by trying to see the other person's point of view. Think not about me, but about you. President Kennedy saw the importance of giving and not taking when he addressed the American people: *Ask not what your country can do for you, ask what you can do for your country.*

Everyone thinks what is happening to them is new. It is for them, but rest assured it has happened before, the only difference is we have more destructive tools at our disposal. Once upon a time bullying and name calling in the playground remained in the playground, now abuse can be circulated instantly and widely by mobile phones and even be spread nationwide through the internet. There was a time when we only had clubs to attack one another, now we have nail bombs and nuclear bombs. We are still doing the same thing: harming another person and the motivation always returns to greed, anger, jealousy and, the old favourite, ego.

This is not peculiar to Britain, everyone is at it, chipping away at someone else's world, character or property; undermining, challenging or coveting. Every nation has their favourite scapegoat or butt of jokes, but as we all take ourselves so seriously these days the jokes can now be interpreted as racism.

Maybe we should put religion and race to one side and think of plain commonsense. Let us be brutally practical about life. When one company acquires another or merges, there is usually what they call a synergy, a complimentary element about both businesses which makes sense of the deal. By combining the two operations distribution networks can be merged instead of being duplicated, accounts and admin departments can be streamlined. The two boards of directors assume that the net result will be a more efficient operation, a better product. By not talking to each other, in fact by being positively hostile towards one another, we will never develop a united country wherever it might be. We will go on wasting our resources. By being antagonistic towards our neighbours we are wasting our energy. By cooperating about trimming the hedge between our two homes we can both be happy and allow sunlight into both gardens. You may think such matters are insignificant in a world of bombing and hatred, but in the real world of daily, mundane life such trivia can quickly escalate. If it is so easy for a man to murder his daughter for kissing a white man in the name of honour, what else would he be prepared to do?

When the first immigrants arrived in the UK they got down to building a future for themselves and their family. Their hosts were mildly amused by these colourful looking characters and were happy to have them in the country because they undertook many of the menial tasks. For a brief moment you could say everyone was satisfied. But being human we did not remain satisfied, that is what Christians call the Curse of Adam. The Asians wanted more and they wanted to bring their families over. The British wanted less; fewer immigrants taking jobs, houses and spaces in hospitals and schools.

The commonsense approach is to accept that we are all here together; let us share our talents and our knowledge as a first step and then try to learn about our cultures and heritage. It should be a merger not a hostile takeover.

An agony aunt always tries to find common ground. This has to be the starting point whether one is trying to solve a dispute or help someone find a marriage partner. There also has to be a willingness on both sides to succeed in the endeavour. One girl wrote. She was angry with her parents, a potential spouse and life in general: *My parents started showing me young men when I was twenty-four years old and even before this when I was at University. It has taken twelve long years. I think I have behaved like a sensible Indian girl who has been brought up carefully by my parents. I must have seen dozens of young men. They were disappointing people but there was one nice one. But nothing happened. A couple of years ago my father suggested a solicitor and got me to agree to see this person. My parents telephoned his parents and they all were very happy to get engaged. I had to force myself to agree as he seemed to be a gentle and very intelligent person. I agreed to meet him. In the meantime I made myself prepare for the wedding which was not easy. In our second meeting, this person suggested that we keep meeting at least for a year, then decide to get married. I was devastated. A year to go on meeting and not get married. I cried for days. I blamed my parents for all this. I was furious with my parents who had raised my hopes.*

Was any one individual to blame? No, it was a combination of circumstances; both sets of parents were eager, the girl had accepted the boy and was prepared to allow love to grow but clearly the boy himself was not ready. It was no-one's fault. If a marriage or a merger or integration fails looking for someone to blame will only result in complete breakdown. Marriages, even those based on true love, have to be worked at particularly in the later years when the physical aspects of married life no longer play an important part. Integration could probably be equated to an assisted marriage; this is not love at first sight but two groups have ended up together for whatever reason and they have a choice. They either learn to respect, perhaps even admire, each other or they break up in recrimination and possibly hostility. Britain in the early part of the millennium is going through a bad patch in its relationship with not just one but several partners. The crockery is flying and voices are being raised. It is time for calm and commonsense to be restored. It is also time for the political equivalent of an agony aunt to speak sternly and clearly when they see wrong before their eyes.

Chapter Fifteen

Now is the hour

We always have a choice in life. Parents can either choose to help and assist their children while respecting their final decision or they can try and force their children to do their will. Children can choose to rebel, to reject their parents or they can choose respect, love and support for their parents acknowledging that there are two points of view. Religions can accept that none has the right answer for all and can choose to explain calmly and intelligently or they can choose the path of hatred, condemning all non-believers as heretics or infidel.

So often, I have had people, young and old, sitting in front of me faced with seemingly insoluble problems; often they are bent on some firm course of action and nothing will dissuade them. Elopement, divorce, abortion. Every day we are all faced with a decision about how to react to a particular set of circumstances or person. As I write these words the UK seems to be living in constant fear of terrorist attack and commentators and politicians, and people in pubs are reacting. We are taught in Indian scriptures that this is the conflict between *Kama* and achieving the knowledge of enlightenment or understanding self, the *Atman*.

Kama is our selfish side, only seeking to do and achieve what will help us personally without a care for our fellow man; it is the relentless pursuit of money, of territory, getting our own way. It blocks out the real understanding. In the *Bhagavad Gita*, the ancient Sanskrit text, Sri Krishna says:

> *Just as a fire is covered by smoke*
> *and a mirror is obscured by dust,*

just as the embryo rests deep within the womb,
knowledge is hidden by selfish desire.

The first and hardest step in resolving an argument or impasse is to let go of all our prejudgements; to let go of our anger, our jealousy, our suspicion and even to let go of self. Take the ego out of the equation as I have mentioned and then start looking for answers.

This is not a softly, softly approach; it is the start of finding real and lasting answers. It is the start of hearing some home-truths spoken with firmness not in a spirit of revenge but with the ultimate aim of finding a lasting answer.

I will say bluntly to my clients that they are being jealous or suspicious and that they can bring the matter to a head by bringing their fears out into the open and talking about them, not allowing them to simmer until they finally come to the boil. If the suspicions are well founded then act swiftly and decisively: the husband must choose between his mistress and his family, he cannot be allowed to get away with it. If a daughter wishes to marry an Englishman, discuss the matter positively without prejudice, without selfish thoughts about the family, and all parties should be aware of the consequences. Once the decision has been taken support it wholeheartedly.

How can we apply this approach to the baffling conundrum of racial integration? The answer is easy, the application is tough.

The first essential is to evaluate the problem. We have discussed in detail the challenges we face to achieve integration, social cohesion or simply basic understanding. I would summarise these as:

> RACISM
> CULTURE
> TRADITION
> LANGUAGE
> RELIGION
> EDUCATION

COMMERCE

ISOLATION

ENVY

With a list like that it would, at first sight, seem an insurmountable set of obstacles. How can any one person let alone a government or governments collectively overcome them? You are right the challenge is too big, there are simply too many issues and sub-issues perhaps even to comprehend. So what is the answer to the question, how do we integrate?

As you may have realised from the earlier pages, I firmly believe that the root cause of any problem is actually the last bullet point – envy or ego if you like. But I will quickly review the others.

Why do we have *racism*? I suspect it is fear of the unknown. We do not know who these foreign looking people are. We do not like the way they dress, the way they eat, the way they smell, the way they behave. We resent the fact that the public swimming pool and gym is closed for one day a week so Muslim women can use the facilities. We think they treat their women badly, we think they are aggressive, snobbish, slovenly, lazy, greedy. We think they are scroungers, we think they are disrespectful of our traditions, of our culture, or our faith, of our freedoms.

In short there seem to be so many reasons for us to dislike one another that it is inconceivable that we could like everyone – so don't try. If you are English you don't even know most of the people in your local village or town let alone city never mind trying to like each of them. But you would not say you actively dislike them for any of the above reasons. At the very least, you tolerate them. You would not sneer at them when they got on the bus or the train. You might even offer your seat. But would you offer your seat if a lady were covered from head to foot in a black dress, eyes hidden by a veil? Or would you wonder why this strange apparition had suddenly disrupted your life by daring to get on your very own bus? I'll explain how to handle the situation in a moment.

Let's take another point – *culture*. It goes without saying that no outsider can ever really understand our culture. After all it is steeped in our heritage, we go back generations. Really? How pure is our culture – in any country? Saudi Arabia is simply a kingdom established as recently as 1932 by a powerful tribal leader who declared himself king and ruler over all the people under his control. The United Kingdom was once not so united. People may call themselves Anglo-Saxons which simply celebrates the invasion of this land by Angles – Germanic people from a district located in Schleswig-Holstein. So it is true to say we have our customs and our habits but it is equally true to say that those have evolved over time, some quite recently.

Tradition falls into the same category; we traditionally do one thing or another but traditions all pass and evolve. It is traditional to pass port to the left round the dinner table, but it will taste the same whichever direction is travels. At the other extreme we struggle to remember why we are marching in a parade but it is what we do every year. There are lots of smiles, the children enjoy taking part, the drums banging and the whistles blowing, but are we in fact commemorating some atrocity, a battle or just long-forgotten grievance? If some traditions cannot stand the scrutiny of critics they will fail; for example should boys and girls, men and women be allowed to mix freely and openly or should women be sheltered from the gaze of men other than their husbands; should women be forbidden from driving; should women not be allowed to inherit the English crown if they have a brother?

Language – this is so often used to beat foreigners about the head. They cannot be truly English because they cannot speak English properly. They may even have failed some English language points scoring system which 'proves' how English they are. Where does that leave all those 'English' natives who struggle to put a coherent sentence together or as Henry Higgins said in 'My Fair Lady', 'Whose English is painful to your ears?'

Religion – how can something so essentially loving be a cause of so much suffering down the ages? Some people believe fervently in their faith, some are not such diligent followers and other people do not believe there is anything at all after we die. The only certainty is that we will all die and that no one can prove conclusively one way or another what follows death. The jury as they say is out and will remain out forever more. So why do we fight so hard to protect it or to destroy it? Why do we mock it if we really do not know, why do we threaten those who remain unconvinced or even are passionate believers in some completely different religion? Some religions are steeped in ceremonies and elaborate rituals, others are very simple, devoid of any fineries or decoration; some faiths have strict teachings and rules of conduct and others have very little in the way of dogma. Everyone must find their own path but on their journey accept that other travellers will be following a different route; or perhaps we could simply follow the advice of – believe in God, beware of religion.

Education – this at its most basic is man's desire to find out, his natural inquisitiveness. Nothing should be off limits and if we try to put a spin on the information the truth will surely come out. It always does. I was condemned for polluting minds when I started writing about sexual matters in magazines and newspapers, now I receive awards. Should religious instruction only be in faith schools? Should there even be faith schools? Are they a contradiction in terms being selective in their beliefs to the exclusion in some cases of all other teachings? The best teachers in schools do not see getting their young students through exams as the be all and end all. Their aim is to open minds and make them receptive to information, to instil in them a passion to learn. If educationalists stifle or corrupt those minds, refusing to show them all the information so the students can form their own opinions then, in my view, they are failing in their vocation to teach.

Commerce – money makes the world go round and for so many it has become their god; my fellow Indians I regret are obsessed with gold and jewellery. One of the biggest money spinners is the arms trade and every country in the world is at it to a greater or lesser extent. Some say there are around 40 wars or armed conflicts going on somewhere around the world at this very moment. The Stockholm International Peace Research Institute Yearbook listed 31 major armed conflicts in 27 countries in 1994. So who puts down his gun first? I mention war in this context because so much of business resembles a battlefield and sadly so much of our personal lives are minor skirmishes too. We all want to be a winner; we are always trying to get something we haven't got – territory, a company, someone else's wife. Morrie Schwartz, the dying college professor, gave a fine explanation in *Tuesdays with Morrie* by Mitch Albom: *Wherever I went in my life, I met people wanting to gobble up something new. Gobble up a new car. Gobble up a new piece of property. Gobble up the latest toy. And then they wanted to tell you about it. 'Guess what I got? Guess what I got?' You know how I always interpreted that? These were people so hungry for love that they were accepting substitutes. They were embracing material things and expecting a sort of hug back. But it never works. You can't substitute material things for love or for gentleness or for tenderness or for a sense of comradeship. Money is not a substitute for tenderness, and power is not a substitute for tenderness.*

Isolation – is another word for loneliness. You can be lonely in a crowded room or town or community. If you really want to live as one 'tribe' that is the most natural thing in the world to do but the time will come when you want to 'trade' with the neighbouring tribe. For now Britain is full of small and large tribal groups who, for one reason or another, do not want to go outside the safety of the commune. But soon we will.

We can, of course, be lonely as individuals. Wives can be

lonely in a home full of young children; they could be yearning for adult company, counting the moments for their husband to return home. But when he gets home late, tired after work, he can only think of resting not about what might be on his wife's mind. How can she be lonely, I am sitting here? You may be there physically but not spiritually. What has her day been like? What has she been thinking about? Even, what would she like to do? The struggle for integration, for really being together, cannot possibly work if we are apart as individuals in our own homes.

Envy of one sort or another will influence all these things. Greed is another word and where you have envy and greed together you very soon get anger. Why should that person have so much wealth and property? The rich should share what they have got with us poor. Again the curse of Adam, we are fated never to be content with our lot.

You cannot take the 'human' out of human nature so our only hope is to work with it and here is the first part of what I could call a four part solution to our differences. We should simply acknowledge and accept that we are different. We are happy for our friends to be different in their likes and dislikes, habits and hobbies. So why not start by accepting that Arabs, Asians, Chinese, English, Poles, etc., are all different. Do not try and change them.

So how do we proceed in a world where we do not trust one another, maybe even do not like one another? These are the steps which I believe will lead us away from dead-ends and potential conflict.

1. DO NOT TRY TO INTEGRATE
Surprisingly, I believe this is step one to developing a more cohesive, balanced and contented society. You achieve integration by not deliberately trying to integrate. By saying people are different and must all be the same, all adopt one another's ways, only follow the ways of the host nation is a dead end street. It

will never succeed, so do not even try. It is perfectly normal to be different. If we do not insist on our friends being like us, why insist on strangers becoming our clones?

Why should we be surprised that Arabs dress differently? Why should we care if they want to cover themselves up? If they want to participate in activities with the rest of the community where to wear a veil would be inconvenient, awkward or possibly dangerous, then they should accept that that is the norm. It is not disrespectful, it is just the way these things are done. Some Sikhs wear turbans, but not all. If possible that can be accommodated, where it cannot the turban should be, and is, removed with the hair tied back. If communities choose to live together that too is fine but they must remember that they are living in Great Britain where British rules apply; they are not living in India or China and no section of town or neighbourhood is off-limits to anyone else. So if that mythical lady should get on your bus shrouded from head to foot in a black veil, help her if she is struggling with her shopping or pushchair. Reject those disapproving thoughts going through your mind. If she chooses to dress like that we should have no complaint. Is she really any worse than the apparition behind her with a stud through her nose, her hair the colours of the rainbow and her iPod blaring so loudly everyone can hear it through her earphones?

History shows that all peoples adapt and evolve. They either absorb the 'invaders' or gradually the host nation adopts the ways of the invaders. As the immigrants are being invited to the UK, they should be welcomed and allowed to settle where they feel most comfortable. One of three things will then always happen. They will either conform with the 'way things are done', they will leave or they will influence the host by their customs and habits. America – the classic 'melting pot' of the world – has a nation of 'Americans' who have a multitude of origins. Many follow different faiths, wear different clothes and look completely different, but all consider themselves American. Indians and Pakistanis, many of whom may have lived in the UK all their lives, still think of themselves as Indian or Pakistani. You cannot make people 'feel' anything; just because they speak the Queen's English impeccably or even cheer on the English cricket team does not make them feel English. In their heart of hearts they feel Asian but at the same time they may hold a British passport as their parents and even grandparents may have done before them. I would say that is absolutely acceptable for the very simple reason that there is no way that you can force someone to change what they feel at their core.

Just as I have advised countless thousands of young people and their parents not to put up impossible barriers, but to accept what has happened and work from there, so too I advise our government, our religious leaders and our 'whole' community in this country without exception simply to start by accepting that we are different. What is certain is that in time we will evolve and change perhaps sooner and faster than we imagine; the Office of National Statistics recorded that in 2006 one in four babies born in Britain had either a foreign mother or father. The ONS was quoted as saying: That reflects the cumulative effect of immigration over the last 40 years.

2. EXPLORE AND ENJOY THE DIFFERENCE

Once we have lifted the enormous burden of not having to integrate off our shoulders, everything else becomes much simpler. Some Asians will adopt English clothes, some will retain their saris and turbans. Some English will adopt Hinduism or Buddhism or Islam, some will retain their loyalty to the Church of England or Roman Catholicism and others will choose no religion at all. We should be happy that there is variety. We should not be suspicious of the unusual, instead we should be intrigued. Ask our neighbours why do they dress, pray, eat as they do but in a spirit of inquiry and not of hostility and even fear.

Above all there should be no attempt to coerce, proselytise or threaten those who choose to be different; after all it was the English who virtually invented the concept of eccentricity. Asians, Arabs, Chinese, Eastern Europeans all choose to come to Britain because they are attracted by something; refugees and asylum seekers choose Britain for its freedom and safety, others come here for the financial rewards and, yes, others come here to abuse and milk the system. This last group will always surface and they should be dealt with swiftly and forcefully without hesitation; Britain does have to get tougher on all who abuse her hospitality. It is no different from dealing with an errant child. A sharp reprimand stops the wrong-doing in its tracks. If you are seen to be soft or weak it will not be long before the mischief makers will exploit that weakness.

So these are the lessons so far. Once we have learned to accept the reality we can then go on to work with it. We should explore and celebrate our differences. We should learn from everyone we meet and talk to them. Find out what they are thinking and why. They may be right sometimes and we may be wrong. One or both may have completely misunderstood: no I do not have dozens of children, but I do live in a large house with an extended family because that is how we live. We believe in the family structure.

I certainly do believe the old adage that if a day goes by without learning something, it is a day lost, otherwise what are we doing? We are vegetating and we are self-satisfied. We know it all and we cannot learn anything from anyone else. The danger here is that we become so self-absorbed that we are incapable of looking up and seeing the world around us. We cannot escape from that famous ego-cage until one day we suddenly realise that our neighbour is doing better than we are. We become envious and angry, we begin to fear that maybe he will buy the property next door as well and then what will happen to the neighbourhood? Is this really so different between countries?

Bullets did not bring down the Berlin Wall or defeat the vast Soviet Union. Eventually people realised that it was better for everyone to work together. Of course it is not a simple route, there is much time to make up, but we have got time. Better that then the alternative.

The Koreans are a divided people, but they are the same. Today in Britain we are a divided society. We are divided along racial lines and religious lines but we have our humanity in common. We all know the dam has burst and we have all noticed our feet getting wet as we walked through the flooded streets. But like the water taking the path of least resistance we have not concerned ourselves with the danger because we live on a hilly part of town. However the water has now begun to lap at our doorstep and there is a very real danger that the house might be flooded. Who is to blame? The people who built the dam with weak concrete and cement, the council who should have put in better defences or at least should have warned us about the approaching danger?

There is no point allotting blame. The damage, if you want to put it that way, has been done; let us focus on recovery. Should the West have supported Saddam Hussein in his war with Iran, should the West have supported the Mujahedin in their war in Afghanistan against the Russians, should the British governments have allowed so many immigrants into the UK? Many thousands of words have been written on the rights and wrongs of all those actions, but the dam has burst, it is time for action. We can, of course, choose to do nothing, which in itself is a positive decision. We can carry on allowing new visitors into the country and watch as they settle in their own communities; some will prosper and some will fail. Things will change.

3. SHARING

Now having learned to accept and enjoy our differences we can tentatively move to our next step and begin to share and exchange our knowledge. To illustrate the point of how fierce opposition can eventually be turned to understanding and acceptance, I quote Nikolaos Provatas, Associate Research Physicist, Departments of Physics and Mechanical Engineering, University of Illinois, in his writing about literature and the arts in Constantinople: *The earliest Christians avoided the worldly learning of the Greeks with their 'philosophy and deceit', and saw no way in which the blasphemous literature could be brought into any sort of relationship with Christian teaching. This reaction of many Christians, as late as the second century, could be summed up in Tertullian's famous phrase, 'what has Athens to do with Jerusalem?' In time, however, Christian thinkers began to realize that there was much to be carried over into Christian teaching from the classical Greeks. Socrates and Plato, for example, often seemed to approximate Christian thought. Likewise many of the writings of Aristotle could be fit right into the teachings of the Church. Indeed after the adoption of Christianity people such as St. Basil and the other fathers of the Church, all trained in Greek literature, were able to show that Pagan literature contained a wealth of teaching that was in accord with the philosophies, dogmas and symbolisms of Christianity.*

Just as a child learns from his mistakes and scholars learn from even vociferous debate, every culture learns from those with which it comes into contact. There is no choice in the matter. You cannot fight it anymore than you can fight for it to happen. Music and the arts are powerful instruments to draw people closer together. Sometimes we just like the tune even if we do not understand the words in a foreign language, but it is the first step in attraction. Worldwide events like Live Aid raise the profile of serious issues through music and raise enormous sums of money and they do that by uniting people first through the music and, once united, by giving out a single, clear message; it might be poverty in Africa, the dangers of AIDS, or to support some stricken part of the world.

Music, dance and literature also transcend boundaries or divisions. Whatever our colour or creed we can enjoy a good play or book. The point is there are so many ways that we can share our knowledge and information and there is so much that we do not know that we have no excuse not to find out. Humans are instinctively inquisitive but we have allowed that gift to atrophy; it is easier to dismiss someone or some group categorising them as 'a bunch of Pakis' or 'stuck up English' rather than make the effort to explore, inquire, discuss and share. But try we must and that brings me to the final step.

4. STAYING POWER

Once we have learned to acknowledge that it is perfectly possible to make progress without having rules forcing us to integrate and that it is perfectly normal to be different without becoming suspicious then we can celebrate and enjoy the distinctions which make us special. But we must have the resolve to stick at it.

Accepting our differences is just the beginning – we have to take all the steps and we have to try harder. This is no different from a personal difficulty between a couple or within a family. Life is not fair, it is full of trials and challenges and the only way to overcome them and succeed is through perseverance. We have to be determined to overcome the setbacks when they happen because they will. For a country the challenges can be enormous – war, famine, flood, terrorist attacks – and the safety and security of a nation depends on all people following the rules of the country; those who do not comply or who are perceived to be a physical threat to the rest of the community should be dealt with firmly.

Setbacks, however, can be on the lower levels; they can be snubs, they can be rude remarks and these are sometimes the hardest challenges most of us will face from outsiders. As it always is in life the young have the opportunities and also the challenges. A 22 year old fresh out of university with a good degree and a job lined up said quite simply – there is no integration. He said that people of different races were friendly in work or study situations but outside the blacks mix with the blacks, the Asians with the Asians and so on. He seemed to have accepted that as a fact of life. My advice to him and all his generation is not to despair and not to try and force the issue. With determination and resolve the changes will come. And it is vital that we should all ignore the setbacks because they too will occur.

So this is our challenge, not just for our country but for all countries and the burden rests squarely on our individual shoulders. It is no good blaming our politicians, or the immigrants, or the neighbouring country – all individual people have an obligation to reform our ways.

We have to let go of our prejudice which more often than not is born out of ignorance. Instead of condemning people out of hand, try to understand what is making them tick, what about you is upsetting them. We have to let go of our self importance which all too quickly leads to anger because of some perceived slight. Maybe we were treated badly, maybe we were barged out of the way as we struggled down the escalator in the underground. Did the man in a hurry do it because he was irritated that we were taking so long or because he just didn't like the colour of our skin, or had he just been told that his wife had been in an accident, had been rushed to hospital and he was trying to get there as quickly as he could? We have to let go of religious prejudice for the very simple reason that no-one knows which, if any, is the true path. We always have a choice. There is always an alternative.

I will not live long enough to witness how Great Britain changes. The scientists say that in time the very physiognomy of the English man and woman will become slightly rounder and slightly darker. One day there will probably be a Prime Minister of Asian origin. A new religion may emerge representing a blend of Hinduism, Christianity and Judaism or some other. It is perfectly possible. Sikhism began only some 550 years ago because Guru Nanak felt there was something missing or deficient about the other religions he saw. In his view people were making mistakes. He thought the way women were treated in Indian society was a mistake; although born of high Kshatriya caste, he considered that the caste system was wrong. He wrote:

No one is my enemy
No one is a foreigner
For me, there's no Hindu, no Muslim
With all I am at peace
God within us renders us,
Incapable of hate and prejudice.

Let me put all this into a few sentences. If we choose to do nothing about the tensions which undoubtedly exist between and within the various communities which now make up the United Kingdom, we can. To hell with the consequences; may the best man win. That I believe is the route which leads to conflict. The strongest may well win but that does not necessarily mean the best.

Alternatively we can be proactive and push the agenda of integration; we can, as it were, try and make people get along. Part and parcel of that, it seems to me, is to be non-confrontational, trying not to upset the apple cart; walking on egg shells or whatever other softly-softly metaphor one chooses. In my view that is also doomed to disappointment and ultimate failure. It will create animosity and friction. 'We don't like that lot and why should we. Look what they have done to our country. Listen to the aggressive tone of what they say and write about us.' I read that there was disappointment that there were no black faces when Gordon Brown announced his new cabinet after becoming Prime Minister. Trevor Phillips, the chairman of the Commission for Equality and Human Rights, was reported to have threatened to resign and be 'hopping mad' not just because of the composition of the cabinet, but also because the issue of equality appeared to be increasingly overlooked by the government. We are back to square pegs in round holes. You cannot force people to be accepted into particular jobs otherwise they become the 'token' minority face with little understanding of who or what they are beyond the colour of their face; they look Asian but are they Indian or Pakistani, are they Muslim or Hindu, are they Indian Muslim or Indian Hindu, can an Indian be a Muslim, can we have both in the cabinet or committee, will there be friction? Believe me there is an astonishing amount of ignorance at the most senior levels in public life about the minority populations. They do not understand because they do not spend any time together; and the fault lies in both camps.

This leads to the third option, the option of choosing not to force the process of integration but, rather than do nothing, be prepared to accept that we are all different and that we can learn from one another. We should be inquisitive and inquiring. Try to understand why our neighbour is angry. And finally we should stick at the task, persevere with our own personal mission to understand. It is possible for one single individual to make a difference because he or she will influence others. Remember the butterfly effect? Can the beat of its wings create a tornado on the other side of the world? I'll leave that to the scientists, but there is absolutely no doubt of our 'sensitive dependency' on one another. If you get angry you will upset someone else who in turn will take it out on a third person. An act of kindness however will have a much more beneficial ripple effect.

The challenge which underpins this final option is to challenge ourselves. We must fight the temptation always to think of number one; it is not so much a case of turning the other cheek and taking a beating, it is to say, help me understand. That is being proactive. Our ego is the most powerful weapon which can be used against us and the irony is that it is our finger on the trigger. It causes us to fight our own corner without pausing for a moment to consider another argument. It stimulates our appetites for money, food, water, energy, property even the very air which we breathe. We always need to have more and we are blind to the evidence that sating this appetite for a while will only make our desires grow.

To my fellow Indians who have chosen to live and adopt Great Britain as our home I would urge them to think again when they say 'We do not need you anymore'. The reality of life is that we do need each other; the success of our country and that of other countries is absolutely contingent on our neighbours.

To my kind and generous hosts for so many years – most of my life – my thanks but also one small request. Open your hearts and minds to all these people you have invited to your land. Try to understand our funny ways and we will endeavour to understand yours. In time, long after I am gone, I hope we will all be much closer together having learned to share and enjoy the very best of all cultures. We can never achieve that if we feel apart, somehow compelled to live in isolation. How can we possibly understand the riches of one another's history if we refuse to explore, to discuss and to share? I am in my eighties now and still feel there is so much for me to find out, often from the very people who come to my door in search of answers to their own problems. There is a wonderful northern England saying: *There's nowt so queer as folk.* Indeed, every one of us is an individual and we all have our little idiosyncrasies. If we can stop thinking of each other as groups, communities or races and start treating one another as individuals we will be making great progress.

When I first came to England more than half a century ago, I came with an open mind and found many people with an equally open mind. I tentatively started my yoga classes not really knowing if they would catch on. It was not long before the classes were fully attended by all sorts of people. I remember there was a nun who saw the health benefits and did not feel threatened in any way by conflicts of religion. She came to learn and to extract what she could from the classes. This, in its own very small way, was a sharing of knowledge and experience. She was not about to become a Hindu or a Sikh because she was practising yoga and I was not about to convert to Roman Catholicism but we were both reaching out to each other. That is what I call integration.